THE TECHNIQUE OF THOMAS HARDY

THE TECHNIQUE OF
THOMAS HARDY

By JOSEPH WARREN BEACH
Author of *The Comic Spirit in George Meredith*
and *The Method of Henry James*

"The lyf so short, the
craft so long to lerne"

New York
RUSSELL & RUSSELL

FIRST PUBLISHED IN 1922
REISSUED, 1962, BY RUSSELL & RUSSELL
A DIVISION OF ATHENEUM PUBLISHERS, INC.
BY ARRANGEMENT WITH THE ESTATE OF
JOSEPH WARREN BEACH
L. C. CATALOG CARD NO: 61-14870
ISBN: 0-8462-0120-8
PRINTED IN THE UNITED STATES OF AMERICA

PREFACE

Since the death of Meredith and Swinburne, Mr. Hardy remains the last of the great Victorian masters. His extraordinary charm, together with his significance as an interpreter of life, has attracted many critics to write extensively of him, and especially of his novels. Poets of such distinction as Lionel Johnson and Mr. Lascelles Abercrombie have written beautifully of him in prose; and he has been made the subject of one exhaustive study, especially in reference to his philosophy, by Mr. F. C. Hedgcock, presented to the University of Paris as a thesis for the degree of Docteur ès-Lettres. University professors like Mr. H. C. Duffin, of Birmingham, and Dr. Samuel Chew, of Bryn Mawr, have made elaborate studies, now of the Wessex Novels, now of his whole literary output. The study which I am offering is more special than any of these. It is a study of Hardy's novels almost exclusively in reference to their technique.

Studies in the technique of the novel are, it seems to me, unduly rare. The literary history of the novel has been largely taken up with subject-matter, style, social significance, the differentiae of realism and romanticism. Until the appearance a few months ago of Mr. Percy Lubbuck's brilliant and subtle book on *The Craft of Fiction*, the novel has been very little subjected to that technical study which has been carried so far with the epic, the sonnet, the short story, the drama. By technique I mean the structural art of the novel: the method of assembling and ordering these elements of subject-matter, social criticism, and the like. The novel has been so democratic a medium, so little regarded as anything more than an evening's entertainment or the vehicle of instruction and propaganda, that scant attention has been given, especially in Saxon countries, to strictly artistic standards applying to it. And such standards as have been imported from the continent have reference rather to style—*le mot précis*—or mere truth to nature. These are certainly matters of the first importance; and it would be hard to exaggerate the service rendered to art by Mr. Howells' worship of Balzac or Mr. Moore's worship of Flaubert. But there is a limit to what can be said upon these subjects, and the limit has long since been reached. Only the genius can find a fresh word to say on the subject of realism, romance, or style. Form, on the other hand, is virgin soil; and there is no aspect of novel-writing that more invites to patient and leisurely study.

It is not by accident that the author of *The Craft of Fiction* is one who was a personal friend of Henry James and the editor of his letters. No writer of novels in English has given more attention than James to the question of technique, and probably none has had a stronger influence on the technique of novelists now writing. It was this consideration which led me to make such a detailed study of him in an earlier volume. If James is not a popular story-teller, it is not, I think, because of his preoccupation with form, but in spite of it. The proof lies in the relatively great popularity of Mr. Conrad, who owes so very much to the technical example of James. The case of Mr. Conrad, by the way, shows what confusion reigns in the critical mind in reference to the

technique of the novel.   Mr. Conrad is often regarded as
a novelist who holds our fascinated attention in spite of
his violation of all the plain rules of story-telling.   And
this because he does not always tell his story straightfor-
ward in chronological sequence, and because he so often
interposes the mind of some Captain Marlow between us
and the events of the story!   It is evident how little
attention has been given to the art of telling a story when
critics blame a great writer for employing two of the com-
monest of the methods of the colloquial spinner of yarns
for piquing the curiosity, maintaining suspense, and
creating the illusion of truth.

Far be it from me to suggest that there is some one
sacred method of writing a novel, and to join with those
who, at one time or another, have undertaken to put in an
academic straight-jacket the writer of plays, of epics, of
short-stories!   There are many excellent methods: I am
as well pleased with that of Dorothy Richardson or Waldo
Frank as with that of Edith Wharton; and I find the
diverse methods of H. G. Wells and John Galsworthy
as well adapted to their respective aims as the diverse
methods of Jane Austen and Walter Scott.   But I think
it would be interesting to have these various methods
classified, and in the case of the great novelists, to have
available a somewhat detailed description of their practice.   This is an undertaking especially suitable to the
university teacher and his more advanced pupils; it calls
for all the taste and discretion at their command, as well
as appealing to their special genius for scrupulous and
systematic observation of fact.   And such study would
be well worth while in the present stage of creative fer-
tility and critical barrenness.   For one thing it would

direct our attention to the neglected subject of method. And it would put us in a better position to judge how far this and that novelist has employed method of any kind, and how far he may have suffered from his neglect or gained by taking thought.

In the case of Hardy, the reader must often wonder whether he was a deliberate structural artist, whether the occasional greatness of his work was not rather the result of a technique which came to him, as we say, by inspiration, and whether indeed the unfailing charm of his work, in whatever degree of greatness, is not something independent of questions of technique. Technique is but one of several factors determining the appeal of any writer; and Hardy with his frequent obliviousness to art is a greater novelist than James with his unceasing vigilance. Moreover, questions of technique are so intimately bound up with questions of philosophy and subject-matter that they cannot be considered altogether in isolation. But structural art is a more important matter than it has been generally considered; the work of Hardy, like that of Meredith, suffered decidedly from the typical Victorian indifference to it. And the moral of our present study will be derived in large part from technical considerations; we shall be mainly concerned with whatever principles of composition, consciously held or followed instinctively, we can find in Hardy's novels, great or less great.

J. W. B.

UNIVERSITY OF MINNESOTA
MINNEAPOLIS, MINNESOTA
July 15, 1922

CONTENTS

ART AND CRAFT IN THE NOVELS OF HARDY: FOREWORD

ART AND CRAFT IN THE NOVELS OF
HARDY: FOREWORD

I

The most remarkable thing about Mr. Hardy's novels, for anyone who takes them in sequence, is their extreme unevenness of quality. It is everywhere agreed to rank the author of *Tess of the D'Urbervilles* as the most serious English novelist of his time. No one doubts that he has produced works of noble beauty, has made an illuminating representation of life, has ranged his facts in the light of a significant philosophy. And yet this artist, this philosopher, this scientist in human nature, is the author of works that by their crudeness positively put his lovers to the blush.

It is not merely that he served a long apprenticeship, that he was exceptionally late at arriving at the fullness of power. There is something regular about a slow development in one's art, something legitimate and pleasing to the mind of the critic, who doesn't like to think of such things as coming too much by inspiration. Quite a different thing is the backsliding of an artist who has once found his salvation—the production of greatly inferior work, of obviously less serious work, after he has proved his capacity for the best. We are content to recognize in *Desperate Remedies* the imitativeness, the offer of ingenuity for originality, proper to a first novel. But after he had found his own rich vein in *Far from the Madding Crowd*, to undertake that abortive experiment in "comedy," *The Hand of Ethelberta;* after he had produced the Sophoclean drama of *The Native*, to indulge in the almost childish melodrama of *A Laodicean!* As for *The Romantic Adventures of a Milkmaid*, there is something brazen in coming to us, the connoisseurs, with such wares. Or is it possible that he was not really coming to us, the connoisseurs, but had in mind a quite different market, for which he was fabricating a quite different sort of wares?

What really was the attitude of Thomas Hardy toward his art? What ideals did he actually hold for a novel? And how far was he willing to compromise his ideals for the sake of popularity?

What he thinks of his own work often appears, so far as the exigencies of the trade allow, in the several prefaces attached to the novels in the collected edition or earlier. Of *Desperate Remedies* he speaks very candidly. It was "the first published by the author," and was written "at a time when he was feeling his way to a method. The principles observed in its composition are, no doubt, too exclusively those in which mystery, entanglement, surprise, and moral obliquity are depended on for exciting interest." A similar condescending, or apologetic, tone may be heard in the prefatory notices to many of the later novels, especially those classified as "novels of ingenuity" and as "romances and fantasies."[1] I fancy that Mr. Hardy, if he felt free to express an opinion, would be likely to pass more severe judgment upon certain of his performances than any of his readers.

---

[1] These are two of the headings under which the stories were classified in the collected "Wessex Novels" of Messrs. Macmillan. The strongest of his novels, as well as two volumes of his tales, are included under "novels of character and environment."

It is notorious what a supercilious attitude he has taken, in these later years of poetic production, toward his stories in general. But if he could so far condescend as to distinguish among his fictions, he would certainly express himself more emphatically on the difference between, say, the "somewhat frivolous narrative" of *Ethelberta* and the "stories of more sober design" between which it came as "an interlude." *He* knows!

2

Mr. Hardy seems always to have taken a serious view of his obligations to the truth of human nature. This appears both in the articles on the novel which he contributed to magazines,[1] and in certain prefatory declarations in reference to his own, even his earlier, works. Even in *Desperate Remedies*, with its tangled melodramatic plot, "some of the scenes, and at least one of the characters" were "deemed not unworthy of a little longer preservation." Even in *The Hand of Ethelberta*, while "a high degree of probability was not attempted in the arrangement of the incidents," "the characters themselves were meant to be consistent and human."

But still, so far as the incidents were concerned, a high degree of probability was not attempted in their arrangement; and in general it is clear that Mr. Hardy did not take so seriously truth to event as truth to character. In his magazine articles he shows a considerable indulgence for improbabilities in the plot of a novel, declaring that minute *vraisemblance* is not essential

[1] See especially his article on "The Profitable Reading of Fiction" in the *Forum* for March, 1888.

to a true representation of life. Human nature is human nature, but a plot is a plot.

It is in line with such a view that the author should not think it necessary in every case to invent his own plots. One might think this essential in order that the sequence of events should be precisely what would naturally follow from the characters and the circumstances in which they are placed. But this is not the kind of scruple that troubles an author of Hardy's force in the manipulation of materials. We know that, in the case of at least one of his greatest novels, he did not find his own plot—in *Far from the Madding Crowd*. This fact came out when the novel was dramatized, and it proved to have the same plot as Pinero's play, *The Squire*. Tiresome litigation resulted; and it appeared that the same woman had *sold* the plot separately to each of the two authors.[1]

We may here at least suppose that, if the story was not made to fit the characters, the characters were made to fit the story, and that their acts and the conclusion were duly considered in reference to the proper "inevitableness of character and environment in working out destiny."[2] But there is the case of another more high-handed and supercilious treatment of mere plot in the still more serious work, *The Return of the Native*. We have it from Hardy's own lips that, in this masterpiece, he was deliberately conforming to the taste of the British public by appending to his tragic story a conclusion in which the minor characters remaining on the stage are happily joined in matrimony. The story was

[1] This statement is made in the *Critic*, XLVIII (1906), 293.

[2] Mr. Hardy's own words in the *Forum* article referred to.

originally intended to close with the drowning of Wildeve and Eustacia at the end of the fifth book; and Mr. Hardy directs readers with "an austere artistic code" to "assume the more consistent conclusion to be the true one."[1] But "certain circumstances of serial publication"—presumably the advice of the editor of *Belgravia*—led him to add a supplementary book, entitled *Aftercourses*, which, as Hardy mischievously expresses it in the argument prefixed to this book in the magazine version, "shortly relates the gradual righting of affairs after the foregoing catastrophe." It was a considerable sacrifice to the gods of the mart. To be sure, there was nothing improbable about the marriage of Thomasin and Venn; and the reddleman quite as well deserved the lady by long suit and service as Gabriel Oak deserved Bathsheba in an earlier story. But *The Return of the Native* was a work of such beautiful harmonious design, with the material so cunningly disposed in the five original books, like acts, and the story brought so straight and just to its inevitable tragic ending, that it was a great pity to have the effect impaired by this half-hearted concession of tepid happiness.

Hardy is certainly not given over in general to the convention of the happy marriage as the conclusion of a tale in which, for the entertainment of the reader, the course of true love is made to run not smooth. A review of his plots would show at once his predilection for the period following marriage as provoking the most varied and illuminating display of human nature. As

---

[1] These quotations are taken from Professor Cunliffe's introduction to *The Return of the Native* in the Modern Student's Library published by Scribners.

late as 1880, however, and after the publication of nearly half his novels, he found himself strenuously dictating a narrative "to a predetermined cheerful ending." He hopes that *A Laodicean* may find favor with "that large and happy section of the reading public which has not yet reached ripeness of years; those to whom marriage is the pilgrim's Eternal City, and not a milestone on the way."

It is probable that a large proportion of those who have "reached ripeness of years" will join their suffrages to those of their juniors in favor of stories that picture marriage as "the pilgrim's Eternal City, and not a milestone on the way." And no doubt Hardy was doing well to keep in touch in this respect with the great reading public, during at least the earlier half of his career, while he was making a place for himself. That is presumably the price which most young writers have to pay for the privilege of writing later as they please.

3

And it is clear that Mr. Hardy never did get far out of range of his public.[1] He never—like Meredith—ignored his public; he never—like Mr. George Moore—wrote for a foreign public, as it were; he never—like Henry James—abandoned in mid-career a public whom he had once secured.

[1] Mr. Hardy's consideration for the sensibilities of the public is shown throughout his career by his singular delicacy in the treatment of all that pertains to sex. This is particularly evident in the emasculated versions of incidents in *The Return of the Native, The Mayor of Caster-bridge, Tess of the D'Urbervilles, The Well-Beloved*, and *Jude the Obscure*, as first given to the public in serial form. In *The Return of the Native*, some of the excisions and modifications incident to this process were continued through many years of serial publication. The curious reader

It is clear that he did not disdain the inherited tools of his trade. I will not say that he did not write for an ideal. But he did not set up an ideal without regard for the views of the reading world. He did not live in an ivory tower. The novel he conceived of as a piece of work for the entertainment of readers. He produced for consumption. He was bent on doing good work; but he was likewise determined to make a success.

He was a regular craftsman—like Dickens, working for the success of his popular magazines; like Shakespeare, actor and manager, working over popular plays for the King's Company, having in mind the motley audiences of the Rose and the Globe.

Here was a young man conscious of artistic abilities, but not at first sure in what direction they lay. He was soon satisfied they lay in the direction of letters rather than of architecture. He felt sure he could write novels; but he was not at first sure what kind of novels to write. He had to try out various kinds, to determine where his own vein lay. We must bear in mind that the true art of Hardy is an original creation—and that is something that cannot be hurried into existence. There it lies in the depths of time, in the great mystery of uncreated things. We recognize it now; it seems as

---

is referred to my article on "Bowdlerized Versions of Hardy," dealing particularly with *The Native*, which appeared in the *Publications of the Modern Language Association of America*, XXXVI (1921), 632–45. The alterations in *The Well-Beloved* were noted by Dr. Mary Ellen Chase in her thesis for the degree of Master of Arts at the University of Minnesota; in her subsequent thesis for the Doctorate of Philosophy she made a similar study of *The Mayor of Casterbridge*, *Tess*, and *Jude*. These studies will no doubt be published in substance within the next year or two.

natural and familiar as the forms which have been with us since the beginning of the world. But before it came, no one conceived of it, no one dreamed it—not the author himself. The author himself had to *find* it. And when he did find it, he had to recognize it; he had to have the faith to declare, against the indifference of the world: "Here is a great new thing I have found; here I will rest." How should Hardy have known in advance the priceless value of that "Wessex" of his childhood recollections? How should he have been able to distinguish in that "Wessex" what he actually felt and knew from what he thought he felt and knew, having absorbed it from literary tradition? And when he had actually separated the good new wheat from the moldy grain of traditional art, how should he have found strength of faith at once to hold to the good?

His first novel was submitted to Chapman and Hall for publication; and the author was advised by the publisher's reader—one George Meredith—that, for a first novel, it dealt too much in social criticism.[1] Perhaps it was the swing of the pendulum which led to the writing of *Desperate Remedies*, the first novel to see the light. This appeared in 1871. It was the year following the death of the author of *Bleak House* and *Our Mutual Friend;* and if there were two novels of the preceding decade which had as great a vogue as those of Dickens, they were, I suppose, *The Woman in White* and *The Moonstone*, by Wilkie Collins. Is it any wonder that the aspirant for honors in the novel should have put forth a book in which the principles of

[1] This statement is made by Edmund Gosse in an article in the *International Review* for September, 1901.

composition were "too exclusively those in which mystery, entanglement, surprise, and moral obliquity are depended on for exciting interest"?

The greatest puzzle comes in the years following *The Return of the Native* (1878). The artist capable of producing that strong and shapely work was surely capable of judging it to be his great original contribution to the English novel. And yet we find him, in the five years that follow, turning out, one after the other, and each worse than the other, *The Trumpet-Major*, *A Laodicean, Two on a Tower*, and *The Romantic Adventures of a Milkmaid*. In most of these novels there is a promising subject, and we are led to expect a really significant picture of human nature and the social order. But the possibilities of the theme were generally not worked out, the actual recourse of the novelist being to complicated and melodramatic intrigue. With *The Romantic Adventures* he reached his nadir. In the following years he produced two really fine novels, *The Mayor of Casterbridge* and *The Woodlanders;* but not before 1891, the date of *Tess*, not for twelve years after *The Native*, did he offer any work approaching it in splendor.

Perhaps we should take into account the long illness referred to by Mr. Hardy in the Preface to *A Laodicean*. This illness may be sufficient to explain both the inferiority of that novel and the continued low level of his work in *Two on a Tower* and *The Adventures of a Milkmaid*. But there are other clues equally promising. In the composition of *The Native* virtue must have gone out of the author. One cannot presumably go on producing such work without intervals of rest. Was it not natural, after the strenuous labor on this masterpiece, for Mr. Hardy to turn deliberately to tasks of less exacting nature?

The whole record, moreover, leads one to suppose that Mr. Hardy made a more or less conscious distinction between the demands of his art and those of his craft; and that, in the intervals of his great original efforts, he felt called upon to try out for himself the more customary—not to say shopworn—methods of the trade. The present-day reader, brought up on the greater novels of Hardy, can make no such distinction: he cannot detect good craftsmanship where he does not rejoice in the recognition of fine art. However it may have been in the past, this novelist is bound to find his readers henceforth solely among those who love him for his art; and such readers are sure to regret as a loss to art whatever was written with an eye to the craft alone.

4

Plot was, for Hardy, the one thing needful. Perhaps he thought that was what the public wanted, and perhaps he was right. But that was not all. Plot was, I believe, the one thing essential in his own ideal of a novel. He seems to have read life in terms of action, objective action; in terms of brute incident, things happening. And he craved, moreover, complication of incident, a web of action crossing and recrossing.

He seems to have been strongly under the influence of the older English novelists. His language is conservative, precise, a little cumbrous, a little quaint, favoring in idiom the eighteenth-century writers, or at the latest Walter Scott.[1] He seems to have been very little

---

[1] It is also at times very beautiful, as I shall take more than one occasion to point out.

influenced by the continental fiction of his day.[1] He escaped almost wholly the great contemporary tendency to subordinate incident to psychology. In the code of his contemporaries, there is no greater artistic disgrace than the unexcused emergence of the naked fact. Every fact must give account of itself in terms of character and sentiment. And it is against the code to make use of a major incident where a minor incident would do. But the mind of Hardy is very matter of fact. He is deeply impressed with the objective conditions of happiness. And he cleaves to the school of Fielding and Scott; he employs the large bold stroke. He is not afraid of incident. He has an Elizabethan gallantry in confronting life in its whole range of action and passion.

And he is too often carried away by his audacity. However interesting his theme, however true to life his characters, he insists on embroiling them in action so strange and tangled as to produce on the reader's mind an impression of artificial contrivance. Even in his latest novel of all, if we were not so much absorbed in the psychology of Sue and the aspirations of Jude, we should be inclined to question the plausibility of a plot which takes on so remarkable a pattern as is indicated by the following schedule of parallel actions and recurrences:

> Jude marries Arabella;
> Sue marries Phillotson.
> Jude divorces Arabella;
> Sue is divorced by Phillotson.
> Sue remarries Phillotson;
> Jude remarries Arabella.

[1] Very little influenced, at least, in matters of technique; more so, perhaps, in philosophy and subject-matter, though I do not feel confident even of this.

In *Two on a Tower*, we have a sense of unreality as we contemplate the series of unlucky accidents which prevent the happiness of the leading characters. That Swithin's great astronomical discovery should have been forestalled by about six weeks is quite on the cards for an aspirant to fame in science. That Sir Blount's death should have taken place really six weeks after Lady Constantine's remarriage, so rendering it void, begins to look like a malign arrangement of fate. That she should have learned of coming motherhood just too late to catch Swithin, somewhere out of reach in the Southern hemisphere, looks like an arrangement of the author's. And that she should die of joy at being kissed by her returned lover some years later, when there is no longer any bar to her felicity, is nothing short of persecution.

Mr. Hardy loves in plot the fantastic, the surprising, something to strike the imagination. He is fond of ranging in that neutral ground where irony and poetry join hands, where the circumstances of men's lives combine in patterns bizarre and thought-provoking. His plots are often original to the point of incredibility. And yet he has no scorn for hackneyed motives[1]—those

[1] We have the secret marriage, for example, in *Two on a Tower*, *The Romantic Adventures*, and *The Well-Beloved;* the Squire of Low Degree in *A Pair of Blue Eyes*, *The Woodlanders*, and the little novel, or long tale, called *The Waiting Supper;* the villainous illegitimate son in *Desperate Remedies*, *Far from the Madding Crowd*, and *A Laodicean;* the woman's secret, fatal or otherwise, in *Desperate Remedies*, *Under the Greenwood Tree*, *A Pair of Blue Eyes*, *The Hand of Ethelberta*, *Two on a Tower*, *The Mayor of Casterbridge*, and *Tess of the D'Urbervilles* (see section 5 of chapter viii); the return of the absent one in *Far from the Madding Crowd*, *The Mayor of Casterbridge*, and *The Waiting Supper*, with the theme in *Two on a Tower*, *Tess*, and *Jude the Obscure*.

popular plot-formulas that have piqued the curiosity
and arrested the fancy of readers from time immemorial.
The secret marriage; the "squire of low degree,"
favored by the heroine but not by her parents; the
villainous illegitimate son; the woman's fatal secret;
the return of the absent lover, or relative, thought dead,
to spoil sport for the living—each of these makes its
appearance more than once, most of them three or four
times, in the novels of Hardy.

But Hardy is Shakespearean in his ability to give a
gloss to commonplace action; and he is Shakespearean
too in his faculty of combining time-honored motives in
such a way as to give the effect of novelty, and restore
them to their original power of provoking wonder.
No one need be surprised to find the illegitimate son
to be a villain, not since the son of Gloster practiced
villainy in *King Lear*. But the fashion in which young
Dare leads his father into wrongdoing in *A Laodicean*
is a bright new coin in the story-teller's mint.

5

Mistaken identity, misunderstandings growing out of
the intrigue of wicked men, the comedy of errors, melodrama, detective ingenuity in the unfolding of mysteries,
pursuit and escape in the fashion of the "movies"—
these are all of frequent occurrence in Hardy.[1] But

[1] Complications arising from a want of understanding of the identity
or true relationship or social status of a character are found in *Desperate
Remedies*, *A Pair of Blue Eyes*, *The Hand of Ethelberta*, *The Trumpet-
Major*, *A Laodicean*, *Two on a Tower*, *The Romantic Adventures*, and
The Mayor of Casterbridge; complications growing out of deliberate
villainy or trickery are prominent in *Desperate Remedies*, *The Trumpet-
Major*, *A Laodicean*, and *The Mayor of Casterbridge*. The device of

one may observe a steadily declining use of them in the course of his writing; they are decidedly subordinate after the *Milkmaid*, and are almost wholly wanting in the last three novels.

He does continue to make considerable use of accident and coincidence and of strange fortuitous combinations of event. His lavish use of accident is not unnatural in one of his philosophical bias. He seems always to have been impressed with the ironic tendency of circumstances to thwart the happiness and the good intentions of men; and character and circumstance continue throughout his novels to collaborate in the production of tragedy. But more and more the emphasis is laid upon character as the dominant partner; and circumstance, while it remains of great importance, takes on the scientific and definable aspect of environment and social convention. In *The Mayor of Casterbridge*, Michael Henchard has much to contend with in freakish concatenations of event. But he was throughout the prime mover of his own fate, and he had fairly to reckon with the results of his own violent, jealous, and mendacious behavior. In *Jude the Obscure* the pattern of the plot may seem surprising in its series of parallel steps. But in point of fact, every step is a logical one, the expression of the attitude of the characters at the time to the complicated problem of matrimony— natural, legal, and sacramental; and the whole elaborate

---

the unreliable messenger is found in *The Return of the Native, A Laodicean*, and *The Mayor of Casterbridge*, with variants in other stories. There is much of the comedy of errors in *The Trumpet-Major*. Mystery and melodrama are too common to call for specification. The movie chase is most strikingly exemplified in *Desperate Remedies, The Hand of Ethelberta*, and *The Trumpet-Major*.

evolution was implied in the interchange of position by Jude and Sue. The interest is not in what happens so much as why it happens; the interest is in the problem, and, for once in Hardy, in the psychology. So that, while the plot survives in full vigor, we may observe, in this matter, what may be called an *assimilation* of the plot.

Such an assimilation is to be noted likewise in his use of hackneyed themes. An almost threadbare theme is used in so late and great a work as *Tess*. But it is not there introduced for its own sake, for surprise and complication of plot. Plot is there simply the handmaid of pity, and the human record is as simple and unforced as a melody of Schumann.

Pity is one stage in the substitution by Hardy of a profounder and more humane interest for the interest of mere ingenuity in the manipulation of plot. The first stage was that of irony, as exemplified in *A Pair of Blue Eyes*. This story was evidently written for the sake of its final scenes—the scene in which the rival lovers of Elfride, quarreling over their claims to her love, learn that they have been riding in the train that bears her coffin; and the scene in the vault where they find themselves in presence of a rival of more grounded claims than either, her mourning husband. There is far more than any interest of plot in the backward glance of the author to the earlier occasion when they had met in the vault, "before she had herself gone down into silence like her ancestors, and shut her bright blue eyes forever."

The second stage in Hardy's progress was marked by the discovery of "Wessex," that old world of dream from which the characters speak to us, in grave or humorous tones, but ever with a mellow sweetness, like the flutes and oboes of the Pastoral Symphony. The first employment of this charm in a story of depth and passion was in *Far from the Madding Crowd*, where it seems that Hardy assembled all possible occupations of the countryside to give truth and beauty to his characters, and to reconcile us to a somewhat commonplace sequence of melodramatic incident. The third stage was drama, of which the first and noblest example was *The Return of the Native*. Here the Wessex setting is specialized, and the incidents grouped and limited in such a way as to bring into highest relief a close-wrought and steady-moving drama of conflicting hopes and wills. This is the culmination in his work of elaborate and powerful structural art.

But a further step in art was yet to be taken, in the very self-denial of a greater simplicity. There is an apparent naïveté in the pathos of *Tess* which may signalize an even greater triumph of design than the more obvious contrivance of drama in *The Native*. It is an even more perfect assimilation of plot. And the exclusive concern for truth which is the principle of composition in *Jude* makes even more surely, it may be, for the eloquent simplicity of the most deliberate art.

It will be our pleasant task to follow through the novels of Mr. Hardy this gradual disappearance of the cruder traces of the workshop—this gradual and triumphant subordination of artifice to art. And while we shall have frequent occasion to note in his work a concern for what he may have thought the demands of his craft rather than for what we consider the demands of art, we shall have the gratification to observe that in his most powerful work, in the novels by which he is actually known to the world, there is no such distinction to be made. The moral is obvious: It was not till he had mastered the *art* of novel-writing that he had really learned his craft.

PART ONE: PROGRESS IN ART

I. INGENUITY

The first of Mr. Hardy's novels is a kind of detective story. The last half of the book is devoted to the solution of mysteries in which our interest has been aroused in the first half. These mysteries hold us because they involve a pair of lovers in whose hopes and difficulties we are concerned. The villain of the story has good reasons for preventing a discovery of the facts, and the process of discovery is accompanied by a fierce though mostly silent struggle of the opposing parties. So that it is a detective story of the most exciting kind. In all this the author follows a formula well known to writers like Wilkie Collins, who made brilliant use of it, for example, in *The Woman in White*.

The resemblance does not stop with the general formula. In both books there are three main mysteries, closely connected with one another, all of which receive their solution at the end. In both cases, one of the mysteries has reference to the illegitimate parentage of the villain; another has reference to the identity of a mysterious woman; and a third to the passing off of one woman for another. Not that *Desperate Remedies* is a copy of *The Woman in White*. The particular circumstances are altogether different, and no little originality is shown by the author in their invention and development. But the many points of similarity make clear the type to which we must refer the first novel by the author of *Tess* and *Jude*.

I

The heroine of the story is Cytherea Graye, who has been thrown upon her own resources by the death of her father. The first mystery is in connection with a love affair of her father many years before with a woman named Cytherea, who for some reason had declined to marry her lover. When he later married someone else, it was after his early love that he named his daughter. When Cytherea Graye grows up, she is engaged as the companion of a Miss Aldclyffe, a middle-aged lady who is likewise a namesake of the goddess of Cythera. And the reader is given reason to surmise that she must be the woman loved by the heroine's father. But the mystery of her refusal to marry him is never cleared up till the death-bed confession by Miss Aldclyffe of an illicit affair with an earlier lover and the existence of a son. This confession comes at the very end of the book; and the mystery of Cytherea Aldclyffe and the heroine's father is what we may call the enveloping mystery, in which the others are wrapped up, and out of which they grow.

The other mysteries are in connection with a certain Aeneas Manston, a clever and mysterious man who is engaged by Miss Aldclyffe as steward of her estates. At first he is thought to be a single man; but later he is found to have a wife in London, and she is sent for to live with her husband. By an accident Manston fails to meet her train. She goes to the country hotel; the hotel burns down during the night, and she is thought to have been burned to death. Such is the verdict of the coroner's jury. This is the second great mystery. Did Manston's wife lose her life in the fire? And if not, what has become of her?

Meantime Cytherea Graye has fallen in love with a nice young man named Edward. But great difficulties are put in the way of their marrying, and great pressure is brought to bear upon her to marry the widower Manston. This she is at last persuaded to do. But on the evening of her wedding it becomes known to Edward and to her brother Owen that there is grave doubt as to the death of the first Mrs. Manston and so as to the validity of Cytherea's marriage. The newly married couple are followed to Southampton, and Manston is persuaded to give up his bride.

He now proceeds to advertise for his missing wife. A woman replies, is identified by him as his wife, and comes to live with him as such. But meantime the suspicions of Edward and Owen have been aroused; and in order to determine the exact legal status of Cytherea Graye, they follow certain clues as to the identity of the present ostensible Mrs. Manston. This is, of course, the third great mystery of the story, closely bound up with the second. Is this really the first Mrs. Manston?

The investigations lead to the arrest of Manston on the charge of murder, and the mysteries concerning his real wife and his ostensible wife are cleared up in a written confession of his in prison. It turns out that, on the night of the fire, he had met his wife and, quarreling with her, had accidentally killed her. He had buried her in the wall of a brewhouse. Then after the suspicion of the community had been aroused, he had got a woman who closely resembled her to impersonate his dead wife.

It now remains only to connect these central mysteries with the enveloping mystery of Miss Aldclyffe and the father of Cytherea. The connection is found in the person of Aeneas Manston. He turns out to be the son of Miss Aldclyffe; it was her desire that her son should marry the daughter of the man she loved, which led to most of the developments in the main story.

Manston hangs himself in prison, and the following day his mother dies. And it goes without saying that Cytherea, as Manston's widow in law, inherits the Aldclyffe property, and marries her faithful Edward, who has been the means of saving her from the power of the villain.

2

There is, in this novel, practically no interest in character as such. The interest is in plot—and plot in its barest and most primary form. The entanglement is brought about by deliberate deception on the part of the characters. The central tangle grows out of a question of identity. The principal excitement is found in the resolution of the mysteries.

The reader is chiefly moved by curiosity. The height of interest comes in the chapters in which Edward and Owen are on the trail of Manston, and in which that very clever criminal is trying to elude them. The favored lover wins his lady by detective work worthy of Sherlock Holmes. He gives the reader a real thrill when he discovers that Manston's advertising for his wife was a "farce"—as shown by the fact that he received a letter from the woman whom he was to exhibit as his wife *the day before the first advertisement for his wife appeared in the papers*. Much is made to hang on a photograph of the real wife which Edward sends up from London to Owen to prove the false wife false.

In this matter Manston shows his mettle. He has been trailing Edward in London, and he traces the photograph and the letter through the mail. He manages to fool the postman to get possession of the letter; he detaches the photograph from the card on which it is mounted, pastes on a picture of his false wife, and returns the letter to the postbox. Mr. Hardy is very circumstantial in his account of this performance, and seems to take great pleasure in the legal precision of the narrative.

But Manston had not reckoned with another discovery of Edward's, a poem addressed by Manston to his wife in which he refers to her *blue eyes*. This was inclosed by Edward in a second letter to Owen, of whose existence Manston is ignorant. So that when Owen goes to church to determine whether the present Mrs. Manston is the real one, he has two things to go upon —the evidence of the photograph and the evidence of the poem. The evidence of the photograph is not conclusive as to the color of her eyes. During the service he finds that she is "easily recognizable from the photograph"; but of the color of her eyes he can make out nothing. To determine this matter with certainty Owen is obliged to resort to a trick. He manages to meet her in the church path. But—

He discovered, as she drew nearer, a difficulty which had not struck him at first—that it is not an easy matter to particularize the colour of a stranger's eyes in a merely casual encounter on a path out of doors. That Mrs. Manston must be brought close to him, and not only so, but to look closely at him, if his purpose were to be accomplished.

He shaped a plan. It might by chance be effectual; if otherwise, it would not reveal his intention to her. When Mrs. Manston was within speaking distance, he went up to her and said—

"Will you kindly tell me which turning will take me to Casterbridge?"

"The second on the right," said Mrs. Manston.

Owen put on a blank look: he held his hand to his ear—conveying to the lady the idea that he was deaf.

She came closer and said more distinctly—

"The second turning on the right."

Owen flushed a little. He fancied he had beheld the revelation he was in search of. But had his eyes deceived him?

Once more he used the ruse, still drawing nearer, and intimating by a glance that the trouble he gave her was very distressing to him.

"How very deaf!" she murmured. She exclaimed loudly—

"*The second turning to the right.*"

She had advanced her face to within a foot of his own, and in speaking mouthed very emphatically, fixing her eyes intently upon his. And now his first suspicion was indubitably confirmed. Her eyes were as black as midnight.

All this feigning was most distasteful to Graye. The riddle having been solved, he unconsciously assumed his natural look before she had withdrawn her face. She found him to be peering at her as if he would read her very soul—expressing with his eyes the notification of which, apart from emotion, the eyes are more capable than any other—inquiry.

Her face changed its expression—then its colour. The natural tint of the lighter portions sank to an ashy gray; the pink of her cheeks grew purpler. It was the precise result which would remain after blood had left the face of one whose skin was dark, and artificially coated with pearl-powder and carmine.

She turned her head and moved away, murmuring a hasty reply to Owen's farewell remark of "Good-day," and with a kind of nervous twitch lifting her hand and smoothing her hair, which was of a light-brown colour.

"She wears false hair," he thought, "or has changed its colour artificially. Her true hair matched her eyes."[1]

[1] Pp. 388–90. All references are to the uniform edition of Hardy's novels, published by Harper in America, by Macmillan in England. In the Macmillan de luxe edition the paging is not the same.

It will be clear how much pleasure the author takes
in the material circumstances of plot and counterplot, in
the ingenious process of discovery.

Meantime the mystery of the substituted wife leads
back to the mystery of the real wife and what became
of her. And the climax comes on a black midnight,
when she follows Manston to the brewhouse, and watches
him exhume the body in order to bury it in a leaf-pit
in the park. It becomes exciting indeed when she
discovers that Manston is being watched by another
woman (who proves to be Miss Aldclyffe), and that
they are all being trailed by a fourth person (who
proves to be an officer of the law)! May we not
affirm that Mr. Hardy gave great promise, in his first
novel, of proficiency in the art of Sir Arthur Conan
Doyle?

Next to curiosity, and bound up with this, is the
reader's feeling of suspense over the fortunes of hero
and heroine. This is felt, of course, throughout the
story; but it grows most intense at certain points
where the heroine is in great danger at the hands of the
villain. The first of these is the evening of her marriage
to Manston, when Edward and Owen learn of the
probable survival of the first wife and begin to suspect
that Manston *is* a villain. Their attempts to reach the
married couple in Southampton in time are met by
several untoward accidents—delayed trains, telegrams
not delivered, etc.; and when once they have reached
them, the difficulties made by Manston add to the suspense. At this point one is strongly reminded of scenes
of flight and pursuit nowadays featured in the "movies,"
kidnapped lady and all. The only thing wanting to com-

plete the resemblance is an automobile racing the train
to Southampton.

Still more desperate is the suspense after the scene
of exhumation. Manston has for the moment escaped
the officers of the law; he is maddened by the realization
that the game is up, and that he has never taken
advantage of the legality of his marriage to Cytherea.
He has nothing now to lose; and, disguising himself
as a farm-laborer, he rushes off to the cottage where she
is staying alone with the horrible design of claiming his
conjugal rights. The brief scene that follows is one of
the most exciting ever conceived by an English novelist.
You see the girl hastily bolting the door of the lonely
house against the suspicious-looking rustic. You see
him peering in at the window. The girl recognizes him,
but refuses to let him in. He smashes the windowpane
and starts to open the casement. She slams the shutters
to in his face. He rushes to another window, enters the
pantry, and so advances to the front room. What
follows must be told in the melodramatic style of the
original.

In extremely trying moments of bodily or mental pain,
Cytherea either flushed hot or faded pale, according to the state
of her constitution at the moment. Now she burned like fire from
head to foot, and this preserved her consciousness.

Never before had the poor child's natural agility served her
in such good stead as now. A heavy oblong table stood in the
middle of the room. Round this table she flew, keeping it between
herself and Manston, her large eyes wide open with terror, their
dilated pupils constantly fixed upon Manston's, to read by his
expression whether his next intention was to dart to the right or
the left.

Even he, at that heated moment, could not endure the
expression of unutterable agony which shone from that extraordi-

nary gaze of hers. It had surely been given her by God as a means of defence. Manston continued his pursuit with a lowered eye.

The panting and maddened desperado—blind to everything but the capture of his wife—went with a rush under the table; she went over it like a bird. He went heavily over it; she flew under it, and was out at the other side.

> "One on her youth and pliant limbs relies,
> One on his sinews and his giant size."

But his superior strength was sure to tire her down in the long-run. She felt her weakness increasing with the quickness of her breath; she uttered a wild scream, which in its heartrending intensity seemed to echo for miles.

At the same juncture her hair became unfastened, and rolled down about her shoulders. The least accident at such critical periods is sufficient to confuse the overwrought intelligence. She lost sight of his intended direction for one instant, and he immediately out-manoeuvred her.

"At last! my Cytherea!" he cried, overturning the table, springing over it, seizing one of the long brown tresses, pulling her towards him, and clasping her round. She writhed downwards between his arms and breast, and fell fainting on the floor. For the first time his action was leisurely. He lifted her upon the sofa, exclaiming, "Rest there for a while, my frightened little bird!"

And then there was an end of his triumph. He felt himself clutched by the collar, and whizzed backwards with the force of a battering-ram against the fireplace. Springrove, wild, red, and breathless, had sprung in at the open window, and stood once more between man and wife.[1]

Surely the reader has never encountered anything more sensational outside of a Griffith film.

3

There is little in *Desperate Remedies* to suggest the author whom we admire so intensely for qualities so very different. Mr. Hardy points out, indeed, in the

[1] Pp. 445–46.

Preface of 1896, "that certain characteristics which provoked most discussion in my latest story were present in this my first—published in 1871, when there was no French name for them." He refers presumably to a certain unromantic "naturalism" in the treatment of the passion of love. The presence of this tendency in the germ has been noted by Mr. Hedgcock in his doctoral dissertation on Hardy. But the tincture of naturalism is so slight that it is quite lost, for the ordinary reader, in the great flood of primitive romance.

More frequent and arresting are the reminders of the true Hardy in certain descriptions of natural phenomena, almost uncanny in their scientific minuteness in the notation of fact. Such is the account of the varying sounds caused by rain falling upon various kinds of land and crop, as distinguished by people going by.[1] We have some intimation of the evocative power of nicely discriminated sounds which makes the charm of so much of the master's work in *The Woodlanders* or *The Return of the Native*. And the marvelous painstaking account of the burning of the couch grass which set fire to the Tranters' Inn, occupying, as it does, nearly the whole of four pages,[2] is a somewhat elaborate preliminary sketch for the more effective description of the burning hayricks in *Far from the Madding Crowd*.

Still more suggestive of the creator of "Wessex" is the occasional glimpse of rustic philosophy, as in the dialogue between Farmer Baker and Farmer Springrove as they watch the passing of Manston's coffin. "Now you'll hardly believe me, neighbor, but this little scene

[1] P. 375.   [2] Pp. 201.

in front of us makes me feel less anxious about pushing on wi' that threshing and winnowing next week, that I was speaking about. Why should we not stand still, says I to myself, and fling a quiet eye upon the Whys and Wherefores, before the end o' it all, and we go down into the mouldering-place, and are forgotten?" Such is the proper and somewhat indeterminate sentiment of Farmer Baker. But Farmer Springrove, even more characteristic, in the very act of recommending resoluteness in meeting life, betrays that pessimism which Mr. Hardy seems to share with his rustic compatriot. "'Tis a feeling that will come. But 'twont bear looking into. There's a back'ard current in the world, and we must do our utmost to advance in order just to bide where we be."

But there is not enough of philosophy, of description, or of psychology, to give more than the faintest coloring to the story. It is upon incident and circumstance that the author lavishes his ingenuity.

4

It goes without saying that accident and coincidence play a large part in the action. It is, for example, the accident of Manston's meeting the wrong train that leads to his wife's going to the Tranters' Inn, with the consequent disagreement, the accidental murder, and all the mystery that follows upon the fire and the woman's disappearance. It is the accident of the rector's being twice away from home, when visited by the frightened possessor of the secret, which makes possible the marriage of Cytherea to Manston, with all that follows upon that event. And these are but two out of the many accidents which go to make up the amazing chain of circumstance.

But this is characteristic enough of Hardy at almost any period of his writing. Accident and coincidence are more or less prominent means of provoking action in all his novels. Perhaps, if we looked close, we should find them to be among the indispensables of romance; and conclude that they are only a little more in evidence in Hardy than in George Eliot or whatever most respectable realist in our gallery. In any case we know that it was partly an accident that led to the misunderstanding between Mrs. Yeobright and her son, and so to all the tragedy in *The Return of the Native*. We know that *The Mayor of Casterbridge* is a tissue of coincidence from beginning to end. So that we cannot lay too much stress upon the prominence of this feature in the earliest novel. The great difference lies in its having here no rival or coadjutor in character or environment, objective accident being in this case merely the natural accompaniment of a story in which the interest lies wholly in objective fact.

Much the same thing is true in regard to certain minor peculiarities of technique. One particular variety of accident much employed by Hardy for advancing his story is the conversation—even sometimes the soliloquy —overheard by some interested party. There are many instances of this somewhat crude device in *Desperate Remedies*,[1] but probably not more, or more striking,

---

[1] Overheard conversation will be found, for example, on pp. 175–78, 328–29, 420–22. Information on matters of fact is given the reader in soliloquies on pp. 105, 116, 126; the state of mind of a character is rendered in soliloquy on pp. 170, 171, 173.

instances than in *The Mayor of Casterbridge*. Mr.
Hardy employs unblushingly in the novel machinery
largely abandoned today even by our playwrights,
who have so much more need of it. In these matters
Hardy is but exhibiting in his earliest work certain
mechanical tendencies which he continued to exhibit
pretty steadily throughout his career. They are not
the characteristics for which we prize him. But they
are peculiarly in place in a story which is a matter of
artifice in its main lines as well as in the minor parts of
its machinery.

II. IRONY

Desperate Remedies, we have seen, was notable for plot, and not at all for character. Mr. Hardy's second book, *Under the Greenwood Tree*, was aptly described by the author as "a rural painting of the Dutch school." It makes a great advance in the art of setting, in which he was destined to become so fine a master. But it is so largely wanting in the interest both of plot and of character that we are inclined to look upon it hardly in the light of a novel; and we pass on at once to the next in the series, *A Pair of Blue Eyes*, which has little of the interest of setting, but in which plot and character make their appearance in that intimate alliance proper to the art of fiction at its best.

I

The bond of union here, as so frequently in Hardy, is irony. And whether it be the mere irony of circumstance—the mere pattern of perverse event, with its thwart incidence of lines of destiny—or the deeper irony of character in its interplay with circumstance, there is here a philosophical appeal, an invitation to contemplative regard, not within the scope of mere intrigue and ingenuity of plot.

The story is, briefly, that of Elfride, the daughter of a country vicar, who is first drawn to the young architect, Smith, who has come down to make plans for the restoration of the church; and then, during his long absence in India, falls in love with his intimate friend,

Knight, the man of letters. Smith returns to find himself supplanted by his old friend Knight. In the earlier period Elfride made a secret trip to London to be married to Smith; but repented of her rashness and returned unwed. When Knight and she become lovers, she makes an effort to confess to him the earlier love and the compromising innocent escapade; but she cannot summon courage. And so the facts come to him from another source under more damaging aspect. And, being a man of very strict views, and unable to read her motives favorably, he leaves her. It is more than a year later that, at an accidental meeting with Smith, he hears a true version of the suspicious episode; and Smith in turn has a revival of hope for himself. Each of the men determines to go down to the country to plead his cause with Elfride; and they find themselves on the same train. The two friends put in the time of their journey wrangling over their claims to the girl. They are unaware that they are traveling with her coffin! After they do learn of this circumstance, they go on wrangling over the love of a girl now dead. They are unaware that, since the breach with Knight, she has been married to another man. When the rival lovers visit the vault where she is laid, they find there the kneeling figure of her husband, Lord Luxellian. . . . . And behold, they are no longer rivals . . . . having ceased to quarrel over Elfride of the blue eyes!

All varieties of irony are much in evidence. It is clear that the author regarded the pattern of his plot with the same satisfaction as a designer regards the nicely calculated crossing of bands of color. It is with bold hand that he lays on the irony of circumstance when he "stages" the quarrel of rival lovers on the very train that carries her coffin. And everything seems designed to lead to that final arrangement in the irony of human nature whereby these lovers, who believe they have shared between them all the affections of young Elfride, are shown retreating from the legitimate mourning of her noble husband in the family vault.

> They felt themselves to be intruders. Knight pressed Stephen back, and they silently withdrew as they had entered.
>
> "Come away," he said, in a broken voice. "We have no right to be there. Another stands before us—nearer to her than we!"
>
> And side by side they both retraced their steps down the grey still valley to Castle Boterel.

So it is too in the earlier stages of the story that one traces the hand of the weaver of ironies. It is with sheer aesthetic gratification that one recognizes in some act of Elfride's with Knight the repetition of an earlier act with Smith. Such is the game of chess, and such is the scene of kissing on the ocean-looking rocky seat. In a more fantastic scene we have Elfride discussing with Knight in the church her kissing with Smith upon the tombstone which they see at the moment lit up by the moon in the graveyard outside. And here the effect is heightened by the circumstance that under the tombstone lies an earlier lover still—a lover not encouraged by the girl, to be sure, but still another in the lengthening series, and one who adds his early death to the provocatives of mocking laughter.

Most dramatic and arresting is the chapter of ironies accompanying the return of Smith to Endelstow. Already the heart of Elfride has been won away by Knight, at this time unaware of the antecedent claims of his friend. But she is still feebly struggling to maintain her faithfulness; and on learning that upon a certain afternoon Stephen will be coming up the coast by steamer, she sets out dutifully to the great cliff to watch for the boat "that brought her future husband home." Not unnaturally Mr. Knight turns up to accompany her on her walk. And then we have a piquant situation indeed. Elfride cannot keep steady the telescope with which she is watching the little steamer down below. She has to ask Knight to look for her, and so to receive from her new lover an account of her old one, while he from the boat is watching them upon the cliff. Then follows the accident which determines for her what she has not had strength of mind to determine for herself. Knight loses his foothold, and is in danger of slipping down to the edge of the cliff; and it is only by her resourcefulness and devotion that his life is saved. The rescue is an affair of the highest excitement; he has a very narrow escape. "Knight's eyes met hers, and with supreme eloquence the glance of each told a long-concealed tale of emotion in that short half-moment. Moved by an impulse neither could resist, they ran together and into each other's arms." It is so that mischievous fate steps in to make the new love secure at the very moment that the old love is on the point of being recalled.

We may be sure that the author was fully conscious of the ironic implications with which he has loaded his story. Not content with one love scene with Knight on the rocky seat where Elfride had agreed to be the wife of Smith, he must needs provide a second, in which the man of letters may be made to wonder "if any lovers in past years ever sat here with arms locked, as we do now." It is on this occasion that Elfride discovers in the crevice of the rock the earring she had lost there long before while love-making with Smith, and so betrays herself to Knight. It is by the merest accident that she does make this discovery. "Only for a few minutes during the day did the sun light the alcove to its innermost rifts and slits, but these were the minutes now, and its rays did Elfride the good or evil turn of revealing the lost ornament."

This is the irony of chance pure and simple, and a somewhat mechanical contrivance for carrying on the plot. We need not assume that it was provided for by the author in his original plan of the story. Quite essential to the main design, however, is the arrangement by which the second lover, who supplants the first, is made his dearest friend and benefactor, and one who has been so fervently praised to their lady by the first as positively to make her jealous. The central irony of the whole history, and the root of all the trouble, is to be found in the characters of Elfride and Knight and their being set against each other in the game of love. It is her very innocence that leads Elfride to take such an exaggerated view of her runaway escapade; it is the very intensity of her devotion to Knight that leads her to the fatal vain attempts at concealment. And she has to deal with a man who prizes above all things in a woman "a soul truthful and clear as heaven's light," with a man for whom her one greatest attraction was her freedom from any experience of love. It is such a man who must needs learn that the woman of his choice is guilty both of experience and of deception.

This man whose imagination had been fed up to preternatural size by lonely study and silent observations of his kind . . . . was now absolutely in pain. . . . . That Knight should have been thus constituted; that Elfride's second lover should not have been one of the great mass of bustling mankind, little given to introspection, whose good-nature might have compensated for any lack of appreciativeness, was the chance of things. That her throbbing, self-confounding, indiscreet heart should have to defend itself unaided against the keen scrutiny and logical power which Knight, now that his suspicions were awakened, would sooner or later be sure to exercise against her, was her misfortune. *A miserable incongruity was apparent in the circumstance of a strong mind practising its unerring archery upon a heart which the owner of that mind loved better than his own.*

2

There is in this novel much of the crudity and experimental uncertainty of early work. There are many reminders of *Desperate Remedies*, many traces of the early-Victorian manner. Such is the rôle of Stephen Smith, the "squire of low degree," pretending to the daughter of a gentleman more than usually exigent in the matter of gentility. Smith is obliged to conceal the fact that his father is the local stonemason; and from this concealment follow certain mysteries and misunderstandings neither appropriate to a novel of this character nor of caliber big enough for the genre of Wilkie Collins. In the case of the widow Jethway, again, the young author resorts to a device not worthy of his subject. She is the mother of the young man who—according to her version—has been killed by the hard-heartedness of Elfride, and whose tombstone plays so important a part in her entanglements. She is accordingly the "enemy" of Elfride, haunting her throughout the story.

It is she who is witness of the compromising expedition; it is she who by her mysterious letters makes known to Knight the earlier history of his fiancée; and her timely and melodramatic taking-off (she is killed by the falling of the church tower while sitting on her son's grave) gives solemnity and convincing power to her revelations. She is "a woman with red and scaly eyelids and glistening eyes," who seems to be a creature of darkness and a denizen of graveyards. She reminds Elfride of "Coleridge's morbid poem, 'The Three Graves,'" and she talks the purest language of melodrama.

Even more clumsy and amateurish are those lighter touches which are meant for comedy. The mystery of the loud kiss overheard in the garden and the path worn by footsteps along the hedge is feebly resolved by the secret marriage of Elfride's father. Mr. Swancourt, with his gout, his recurrent story which is "too bad" for a clergyman to tell, and his insistence on providing a distinguished descent for the man named Smith, is a humor feebly in the manner of Thackeray, or Trollope; while William Worm, the "dazed factotum," with his constant complaint of "people frying fish" in his head, is a humor feebly in the manner of Dickens.

There is in this story no little of the objective interest of intrigue. But the main beauty lies in the character of Elfride. She is the first expressive figure in Mr. Hardy's portrait-gallery of women, and one of the most appealing. He does very little with his attempts to describe her looks by comparisons with Raphael, Rubens, and Correggio. He does better with the game of chess in which she finds herself so at the mercy of Knight's superior mind; still better with the earrings that make such an appeal to her womanly love of ornament and such a test of her loyalty; and best of all with her half-truths, and shifty changes of ground when she is brought to bay. Poor little woman—so inexpert, so willing to put off the evil day, so determined at all costs to keep her man's good opinion and his love! Her very inconstancy, her creator would have us feel, was a trait that went with a nature "the most exquisite of all in its plasticity and ready sympathies." We are early prepared for her marriage to Luxellian by her motherly fondness for his orphan children; so that we agree with Knight in putting a charitable construction upon her act, especially as we are made to feel that she died of a broken heart. "Can we call her ambitious?" says Knight to his rival. "No. Circumstance has, as usual, overpowered her purposes—fragile and delicate as she— liable to be overthrown in a moment by the coarse elements of accident."

So the author sounds, in the third of his novels, what is to be a *leitmotif* running through the series that follow. We shall find it in the story of Bathsheba in *Far from the Madding Crowd*, in that of *Tess of the D'Urbervilles*, in that of *Jude the Obscure*. There is nothing that has impressed him more than the fragility of human nature, and its helpless exposure to "the coarse elements of accident."

> A violet in the youth of primy nature,
> Forward, not permanent, sweet, not lasting,
> The perfume and suppliance of a minute,
> No more.

Such is the motto prefixed to the story of Elfride. It is with the elegiac tenderness of a poet that Hardy has conceived this heroine, distilling his sweet essence from the bitter herbs of her unhappy lot.

And from the action as a whole, as from the title of the book, there rises a somewhat more acrid perfume of dramatic irony. It is just a pair of blue eyes that stirs up such a coil; it is just a light bit of womanhood that draws out of their orbits such weighty bodies as Smith and Knight, that causes misunderstanding and separates dear friends. This is no longer the contriver of plots, preparing surprises, with whom we have to deal. This is an artist, pondering thoughtfully the inscrutable and shadowed beauty of men's lives.

III. SETTING

An architect, an editor, a Lord, and the literary daughter of a vicar—Mr. Hardy was never to play his best tunes on such instruments. Much more promising were the characters chosen to carry the leading rôles in his next novel—a shepherd, a rich farmer, a sergeant, and a woman manager of her own farm. And for the thin-bodied minor figures of *A Pair of Blue Eyes*, we have, in the richly furnished background of *Far from the Madding Crowd*, no less engaging a company than that of Joseph Poorgrass, Liddy Smallbury, and Warren the maltster, not to speak of ill-starred Fanny Robin.

I

The story is closely bound up with the normal incidents of country life. The leading man and woman make acquaintance while he is tending his sheep and she is doctoring her aunt's cows. The shepherd helps the milkmaid to recover her hat blown away by the wind, and she reciprocates by saving him from suffocation in his unventilated shepherd's hut. Their first extended conversation—upon the shepherd's proposal of marriage—is introduced by his offer of a lamb for a pet.

His proposal was not made without a certain encouragement from the ingenuous milkmaid. And while she cannot find it in her heart to accept, we are prepared for the lifelong service of Gabriel Oak and for the eventual capitulation of Bathsheba Everdene.

It is true he swears he will never ask her again to be his wife; but that, we feel, will prove no bar to their union.

Bathsheba very shortly leaves her aunt's place to become mistress of a fine farm in the neighborhood of Weatherbury. And a great "pastoral tragedy" reduces Gabriel Oak from an independent sheep farmer to a mere shepherd open to hire. The loss of his sheep sends him on the road to seek for employment; and he happens to arrive in Weatherbury in time to save certain wheat-ricks from burning. The owner is Bathsheba Everdene, who now engages the resourceful Gabriel as her shepherd.

At this point a new character enters the story— rich Farmer Boldwood, a grave, self-contained man, who has never, it seems, yielded to the witchery of woman. He is the sole man not to take notice of Bathsheba when she goes to do business in person at the Casterbridge corn market. He is easily set aflame, however, by a valentine dispatched by Bathsheba in thoughtless mood. It is her levity in the treatment of Boldwood which leads to her first quarrel with Gabriel Oak, who has more regard for her good name than for his own happiness. While they are grinding the shears at the sheep-shearing she asks her shepherd's advice, and gets a scolding, with the result that he is discharged. So indispensable a man as Gabriel, however, cannot long remain under a cloud; and it is only twenty-four hours later that he is summoned back in the most pressing and almost affectionate manner. A great number of the sheep have got "blasted," and no one else can be trusted to perform the operation necessary to save their lives. Indeed Gabriel is indispensable not merely in his capacity of shepherd, but in a general business way, since Bath-

sheba discharged her dishonest bailiff and assumed the
management of her own farm.

But Gabriel is to play a very small part in the story
during most of the middle portion. The main rôles
are carried by Boldwood and by Sergeant Troy, a gallant
and worthless "single man in barracks." We know
that he is the seducer of Fanny Robin, the country girl;
that he has agreed to marry her, but has welcomed
some excuse to put off indefinitely the meeting of this
obligation. Bathsheba knows only that he has a bad
reputation; and she will not believe any wrong of a man
so dashing and with such a command of ingenious
flattery. The most decisive factor in his wooing is his
display of swordsmanship in the hollow amid the ferns,
when he surrounds her on all sides with the rapid,
bewildering flashes of his blade. Such an exciting
exercise of coolness and nerve on the part of both of
them could be followed by nothing less exciting than a
kiss. And that was an experience which "brought the
blood beating into her face, set her stinging as if aflame
to the very hollows of her feet, and enlarged emotion
to a compass which quite swamped thought." The
admonitions of Gabriel and the reproaches of Boldwood,
now beside himself with jealousy, do not prevent the
growth of her passion for Troy. Indeed the fury of
Boldwood actually starts her off to Bath in order to
warn her lover of danger; and it is there that Troy so
works up her jealousy of some woman "more beautiful
than herself" that she marries him on the spot.

Troy proves to be a thriftless farmer, and he wastes
Bathsheba's fortune on the race track. The contrast
of his character with Gabriel's is brought out vividly

in one of the bucolic incidents. It is the time of the harvest festival; and Troy, though warned of approaching storm, has encouraged all the farm hands to get drunk in the great barn, leaving unprotected the wheatricks "with the rich produce of one-half the farm for that year." And so it is Bathsheba and Gabriel who, alone in the midst of a storm of thunder and lightning, perform together the labor of covering the grain.

And now the story comes to a climax with the death of Fanny in childbirth at the Casterbridge "Union," and the bringing of the bodies of mother and babe for burial at Weatherbury. Owing to certain circumstances, the coffin is left in Bathsheba's house overnight; and there it is that Bathsheba, whose suspicions have been aroused by various incidents since her marriage, opens the coffin and makes herself certain of the odious facts. Then while she is there alone, trying to overcome her jealousy of this poor victim of her husband's, the husband comes himself, to make sentimental amends to the dead woman by brutal insults to the living. On both sides it is the end of their love; and having first set up a monument "in Beloved Memory of Fanny Robin," Sergeant Troy now leaves the country, disappearing under circumstances which suggest that he has been drowned.

Meantime, since Bathsheba's marriage, Farmer Boldwood has so completely lost interest in life as to have utterly neglected his farm. But after the disappearance of Troy he begins to pick up hope; and as time passes, he receives some encouragement from Bathsheba, who has come to think that she owes all possible amends to a man she has wronged. It is

Boldwood's modest plea to be allowed to serve for the same period as Jacob served Rachel; and after more than a year, at a Christmas Eve party at his house, she is persuaded to give him her promise that, at the end of six years more, she will marry him. It is only a few minutes later that her husband appears at the party, returning as if from the dead, and summons her to come home with him. In her extreme astonishment she makes no movement to obey; and when Troy reaches out to draw her toward him, she shrinks away from his touch. "This visible dread of him seemed to irritate Troy, and he seized her arm and pulled it sharply. Whether his grasp pinched her, or whether his mere touch was the cause, was never known, but at the moment of his seizure she writhed, and gave a quick, low scream. The scream had been heard but a few seconds when it was followed by a sudden deafening report that echoed through the room and stupefied them all." Boldwood had shot Troy.

The author disposes briefly of the rest of his story. Boldwood gives himself up to justice. He pleads guilty, and is sentenced to death. But owing to certain evidence of insanity, the government intervenes, and his sentence is commuted to "confinement during her Majesty's pleasure." Nothing is now left but to bring about the union of Bathsheba with the first one of her lovers, and the one marked from the first, by character and capacity, as best suited to give her that reasonable measure of happiness which Mr. Hardy accords to his more favored heroines. The other men have served well for excitement and "red herring." And it now remains for the career of our heroine to return to the level of peace and security. But how is this to be brought about when the hero has sworn he will never again pay suit to the heroine? It will e'en be necessary for the heroine to pay suit to him. Gabriel has long since been made bailiff of Bathsheba's farm, as well as being intrusted with the superintendence of Boldwood's. But not having been given any reason to suppose that he might win the hand of Bathsheba, and not liking the appearance of "waiting around for poor Boldwood's farm, with a thought of getting you some day," he has made up his mind to seek his fortune in foreign parts; and a year after Boldwood's Christmas party, he sends Bathsheba formal notice that he will "not renew his engagement with her for the following Lady-day." It is this threat of desertion that fetches her. She comes to his hut virtually in the rôle of suitor. "And quite right, too," says Oak. "I've danced at your skittish heels, my beautiful Bathsheba, for many a long mile, and many a long day; and it is hard to begrudge me this one visit."

2

One would like to know whether, in designing this novel, the author started with a plot and added a setting, or started with a setting and got himself a plot to suit it. My impression is that he started with the setting. He conceived the idea of a pastoral idyll, in which he should bring together the greatest possible number of country scenes and occupations such as, taken together, would amount to a reconstruction of his ideal "Wessex," or—more specifically—of that particular department of Wessex known as "Weatherbury."

Mr. Hardy tells us in the Preface that it was first in this book that he "ventured to adopt the word 'Wessex' from the pages of early English history, and give it a fictitious significance as the existing name of the district once included in that extinct kingdom. The series of novels I projected being mainly of the kind called local, they seemed to require a territorial definition of some sort to lend unity to their scene."[1] He discusses at some length the peculiarities of "the village called Weatherbury," which, owing to the disappearance of many of the customs and architectural features following the growth of migratory labor, "would perhaps be hardly discernable by the explorer, without help, in any existing place nowadays."

We are made to feel that the book is primarily a reconstruction of a "realistic dream-country," and that the plot—which, as we know, was procured from a purveyor of such wares—was introduced as a necessary means of giving coherence to the dream. In any case, it is evidently a composition of pastoral elements very consciously designed. This appears, for one thing, in the classical and biblical allusions, which seem to occur more frequently in this book than elsewhere, as if the author had been reading up his subject in the prescribed poetic manuals. The renewed activity of the vegetable world in early spring makes him think of the dryads "waking for the season." The ballad sung

[1] Much later, on publishing his stories as the Wessex Novels, Mr. Hardy made many minute changes, especially in the greater use of local dialect, by way of thickening the Wessex atmosphere, giving coherence to the whole series, and, as it were, putting his stamp on each member of it. Many instances are given by Miss Chase in her doctoral dissertation referred to earlier.

by Jacob Smallbury at the shearers' feast was "as inclusive and interminable as that with which the worthy toper, old Silenus, amused on a similar occasion the swains Chromis and Mnasylus, and other jolly dogs of his day." Gabriel calling his lost sheep makes the valleys and hills resound "as when the sailors invoked the lost Hylas on the Mysian shore"; and at the grindstone, sharpening his shears, Gabriel "stood somewhat as Eros is represented when in the act of sharpening his arrows."

Some of these allusions seem a little forced, and as if introduced consciously for decoration. More natural and in keeping are the biblical allusions. These are heard not merely from the pious mouth of Joseph Poorgrass, for whom they make the chief trait in his humorous characterization, but also from those of other serious persons such as Farmer Boldwood. Very effective is the author's comparison of Gabriel Oak to Moses on the occasion when Bathsheba sent him off and bade him never let her see his face any more. "'Very well, Miss Everdene—so it shall be.' And he took his shears and went away from her in placid dignity, as Moses left the presence of Pharaoh."

The very names are chosen largely for their combination of biblical and rustic associations, from the archangelic Gabriel Oak, and Bathsheba Everdene, recalling the lady for whom King David sinned, down to Joseph Poorgrass, Jacob Smallbury, Matthew Moon, and Laban Tall. If there is a third range of association to which appeal is made, besides the Bible and the English land itself, it is the imaginative demesne of *As You Like It* and *A Midsummer-Night's Dream*.

But more convincing than literary allusion and the association of names are the actual character and behavior of the people of the story; and these are almost exclusively of the true agricultural, or more specifically pastoral stamp. The nearest approach to the modern industrial order is Bathsheba paying off her men "pen in hand, with a canvas moneybag beside her." And the key to the whole composition is given in the scenes of Gabriel playing his flute in his shepherd's hut as the Grecian shepherds sounded their oaten pipes, and watching the stars and reckoning time from the top of Norcombe Hill as certain other shepherds watched by night in scriptural story. It is a question whether Gabriel or Bathsheba should be regarded as the leading character. As Bathsheba is undoubtedly the central actor in the drama, so Oak is the central feature of the pictorial composition, the poem, to which the drama was attached. We are most interested in the emotional history of Bathsheba, but Oak is the indispensable and characteristic figure in those rural scenes which form so large a part of the design. We see him waking in his hut to take up the new-born lamb revived by the warmth of his fire, or standing sorrowful on the brow of the hill beneath which lie the mangled carcasses of his flock. We see him presiding at the sheep-washing by the pool in the meadows, or at the sheep-shearing in the great barn, or lancing the stricken beasts with his own sure merciful hand to save their lives. And when it was not the sheep, it was the grain which solicited his anxious care. It was he who saved the wheatricks from fire and from rain; it was the trained eye of the watcher in the pastures that read the signs of the approaching storm. It was he who by long-proved competence in affairs, and by tender and dogged faithfulness of heart, amply earned at least the heart and hand of the wayward Bathsheba.

3

All three of the serious main characters, all but the soldier-villain himself, are conceived in the large grave manner of Scripture pastorals. By their comely dignity, by their respect for one another and for themselves, by their direct and deliberate manner of speech and action, they remind us of characters in the Old Testament—in the story of Joseph or of Ruth, of King David or of Queen Esther. There is none of the small change of the modern drawing-room. Their language is worthy of the open air in which they move and the wide horizons on which they rest their eyes. They "deal boldly," like Wordsworth's pastoral poet, "with substantial things." Thus it is that Gabriel delivers, in precise and measured terms, his judgment upon the behavior of Miss Everdene toward Farmer Boldwood. Thus it is that Farmer Boldwood puts away Bathsheba's offer of pity, and wants to know what has become of her seeming promise of love.

"Your dear love, Bathsheba, is such a vast thing beside your pity, that the loss of your pity as well as your love is no great addition to my sorrow, nor does the gain of your pity make it sensibly less. Oh sweet—how dearly you spoke to me behind the spear-bed at the washing-pool, and in the barn at the shearing, and that dearest last time in the evening at your home! Where are your pleasant words all gone—your earnest hope to be able to love me? Where is your firm conviction that you would get to care for me very much?"

It is with the same high gravity that Bathsheba makes her defense to Boldwood, as she had formerly made her defense to Gabriel against similar reproaches.

> She checked emotion, looked him quietly and clearly in the face, and said in her low, firm voice, "Mr. Boldwood, I promised you nothing. Would you have had me a woman of clay when you paid me that furthest, highest compliment a man can pay a woman—telling her he loves her? I was bound to show some feeling, if I would not be a graceless shrew. Yet each of those pleasures was just for the day—the day just for the pleasure. How was I to know that what is a pastime to all other men was death to you? Have reason, do, and think more kindly of me!"

M. René Bazin remarks of one of his peasant characters, "She expressed herself well, with a certain studied refinement which denoted the habit of reading." Something of that sort is true of all the characters of Hardy, especially the main characters in the more serious novels. But it is not the habit of reading that is responsible for this adequacy and propriety of self-expression. It is a certain simple elevation of mind, a freedom from sophistication, and a directness in dealing with solid realities. It is the mutual respect of the speakers born of an instinctive regard for the human soul. This the author shares with his creatures. Whatever may be said of Hardy's irony, his pessimism, his want of religious faith, there can be no question of the dignity with which he invests the human soul itself. The manner of speech of Bathsheba and Gabriel and Boldwood is the manner of speech of Eustacia Vye and Wildeve and Clym and Mrs. Yeobright; of Henchard and Farfrae and Lucetta; of Tess and Angel Clare; even of Jude and Sue. At first it may strike the reader as somewhat awkward and unnatural, somewhat formal and precise, like the expression of foreigners who speak with care a language learned from books. The reader has been used—in books and in daily experience—to a more trifling and more trivial style, the common style of the tea table or the railway train. He must accustom his ear again to the broad simple accents of scriptural speech. He is at first more ready to believe that people talk like the witty fencers of *The Egoist* and *The Awkward Age*, or in the broken sentences and slangy "patter" of the characters of Messrs. Wells, Walpole & Co. But in time one comes to love these squared and grounded sentences, as one loves the large deliberate movements of those who speak them; and one yields with delight to the thought of people as strong and simple as those in Genesis or the *Iliad*, "in the early ages of the world."

This style first appears in all its beauty in *Far from the Madding Crowd*. There had not been earlier any sufficient occasion to draw it out. The slight story of *Under the Greenwood Tree*, a story of boy and girl love, had not depth enough to call for speech of any force or dignity. Neither had the somewhat labored and childish exchanges of Smith and Elfride in *A Pair of Blue Eyes*, nor the shallow literary encounters of Elfride and Knight. But the characters in the later story are given weight and consistency by the obvious importance of the things with which they deal, and the whole action impresses by virtue of the material stakes involved.

Bathsheba is the first of a series of independent Shakespearean women capable of taking strong hold upon life and meeting men upon something like an equal footing. And it is the Weatherbury composition that

promotes the development and display of this superb
character; such character first shows itself upon the use
of the Wessex setting in connection with a real story.
The discovery of Bathsheba in the rôle of a personage
capable of giving employment to the shepherd, her
discharge of the dishonest bailiff and her payment of
the laborers in person, her appearance in the corn
market to do business with men, and at the head of the
table at the harvest festival as patron of the feast—all
these are incidents in building up a personality of unusual
impressiveness. We are prepared for her display of
Roman heroism after the shooting of Troy, when she
took command of the situation with such matronly
coolness, instead of fainting and giving up the guidance
to others. She proved then, as Hardy says, that "she
was of the stuff of which great men's mothers are made."

It is true that, after all necessary steps were taken in
the case of the murdered husband, Bathsheba did give
way to fainting fits, and went to bed; just as after
laboring with Gabriel in the storm till the grain was
practically secured she had consented to give over,
being weary. It is true that, with all her pride and
candor, her fairness and moral responsibility, she became
the victim of a woman's vanity, helpless against the
assaults of gallant flattery; and that, without the heart
of a coquette, she managed to play the rôle of one.
These are weaknesses which detract less from her charm
than they add to her lifelikeness. They are the debt
she paid to nature. They are what she has in common
with Elfride and with the heroine of *Under the Greenwood
Tree*. They are the source of all her trouble and the
mainspring of the plot; and they serve to set in higher

relief her more heroic qualities. It is the strong and the weak in her nature taken together that make her so very real. And yet it is her strength that gives her her special interest; and it is her position of Weatherbury farmer that accounts for the appearance of such a character in English fiction.

It is not necessary to labor this point in connection with Oak and Boldwood. Both of these have much of that generous helpfulness of nature toward the loved one which Hardy is so fond of representing in men of country breeding—witness the self-effacing love of Diggory Venn in *The Return of the Native* and of Giles Winterborne in *The Woodlanders*. The most affecting instance of the tenderness of Oak and Boldwood was their chivalrous conspiracy to keep from Troy's wife a knowledge of the story of Fanny Robin. Such gentleness is particularly natural to the shepherd, with his humane and motherly regard for silly beasts. When he found his sheep all dead at the foot of the fatal cliff, his first feeling "was one of pity for the untimely fate of these gentle ewes and their unborn lambs"; it was only in the second place that he remembered the sheep were not insured, and that he had lost in one night his labor of ten years. Is it any wonder that such a man should have watched so long over his lady's interests as if they were his own, that he should have cared more for her happiness than for his own success with her?

4

The feeling of the characters for one another, as well as their personal quality, is developed by their rural occupations so as to give especial reality to the story.

Mr. Hardy remarks, when he has at last brought about the engagement of Bathsheba and Gabriel:

> Theirs was that substantial affection which arises (if any arises at all) when the two who are thrown together begin first by knowing the rougher sides of each other's character, and not the best till further on, the romance growing up in the interstices of a mass of hard prosaic reality. This goodfellowship—*camaraderie*—usually occurring through similarity of pursuits, is unfortunately seldom superadded to love between the sexes, because men and women associate, not in their labours, but in their pleasures merely. Where, however, happy circumstance permits its development, the compounded feeling proves itself to be the only love which is strong as death—that love which many waters cannot quench, nor the floods drown, beside which the passion usually called by the name is evanescent as steam.

Whether Mr. Hardy succeeded in convincing us of the existence of a love between Bathsheba and Gabriel worthy of such romantic phrasing is a matter of doubt. It is always very hard—as Meredith found in *Diana*—to satisfy the reader of romance with the wise second or third love of a woman who has imprudently dispensed her youthful passion. But however we may feel about the *love* to which the good-fellowship was added, we are made to believe fully in the good-fellowship, the *camaraderie*, which has grown up through the similarity of pursuits of Bathsheba and Gabriel. We are made to realize it in ways much more convincing, because so much more directly appealing to the senses, than in the case of Diana and Redworth. To have saved the shepherd's life was a good beginning. And this was well followed up by her recognizing in the one who played so manly a part at the burning of the straw stack the same who had proposed marriage to her not long before, and being practically compelled, by the general opinion of his merits, to offer him employment. The various incidents of farm life give body and color to their relation, which is not rendered less intimate and binding by the little quarrels arising from his well-deserved reproofs. The scene which more than any other brings them close is that in which they work together to save the wheat-ricks from the storm while the lightning flashes and her drunken husband sleeps with his men in the barn.

Never was growing friendship displayed under more picturesque aspects. It is a wonder the makers of "movies" have not discovered the possibilities of these pictures as they have those of *Tess*. All the while our hero was showing himself the best man in ways equally well approved, in the long run, by romance and real life.

And Bathsheba was playing a rôle not the less convincing for being partly politic. When, after his dismissal, she could not get him to help her with the swollen sheep by oral command, she wrote him a polite note, at the end of which she added, out of "strategy," the more tender appeal, "Do not desert me, Gabriel!" So she played upon his sentiments. And when he had finished his surgery:

> When the love-led man had ceased from his labours, Bathsheba came and looked him in the face.
>
> "Gabriel, will you stay on with me?" she said, smiling winningly, and not troubling to bring her lips quite together again at the end, because there was going to be another smile soon.
>
> "I will," said Gabriel.
>
> And she smiled on him again.[1]

It is true she needed him in a business way. But we cannot suppose that this incident and her strategic

[1] P. 163.

smiles left her entirely without a more personal regard
for the man who was her moral support as well as her
man of affairs. And after the death of Troy and the
incarceration of mad Boldwood, it was by no means
solely the threatened loss of her superintendent that
made her so desolate at the thought of losing Gabriel.
But he could not have played better cards if he had
done it deliberately than to go about his own business
at Weatherbury and make his plans for emigration.
The rest followed naturally; and if it was not *la grande
passion* which led her to the altar, it was at least the
affectionate regard and the feeling of absolute security
with which a woman who has proved the perils and
betrayals of love looks to the man of tried strength and
fidelity.

To one who has read the book there is a smack of
irony in the title. But the emotional strife which makes
up this drama is not the "ignoble strife" which the poet
had in mind; and it may well be that, in choosing his
title, the author had no thought of an ironic bearing.
He intended to compose an idyll of pastoral and agricultural life as he had composed a sylvan idyll in *The
Greenwood Tree;* and he was moved solely by the
sentiment proper to the lovely peaceful life remote from
the insane huddle of the market. But meanwhile, in
A Pair of Blue Eyes he had achieved the construction
of an exciting plot of deeply human interest; and he
doubtless felt the need of introducing in his pastoral
setting a much more gripping action than he had done
in the sylvan one. He had probably been impressed
with the possibilities of the country for moving drama
mentioned later in *The Woodlanders.* And so he

proceeded to secure his plot in the way we have seen, and to adjust it to the circumstances and personal types of Weatherbury life.

It may be that some of the later scenes are of a violence for which we are not prepared; and certainly there is an artificiality in the contrivance of some of the situations which displays the ingenuity rather than the humane art of the craftsman.[1] But if the plot is not at every point made consistent with the original design of the piece, it owes to this original design its general plausibility, its *vraisemblance*, its local color and life. The setting, we may suppose, came before the plot in the author's plan; and it is the setting which "made" the plot. So that we have the emergence of a really convincing and characteristic story simultaneously with the emergence of what we call Wessex. What we call Wessex is an indispensable element in the formula for a first-rate novel by Hardy.[2]

5

What we call Wessex is a composite of many things, a harmony of many traits, physical and moral, human and non-human. It is, in the first place, a physical background of landscapes and interiors, with enveloping conditions of climate and atmosphere. It is next an economic order, a social order, with its well-marked

[1] Such is the amazing scene of trickery in the thirty-fourth chapter, when Boldwood, not knowing of the marriage, is led on by the mischievous cunning of Troy, first to pay him a large sum of money to marry Fanny, and then another large sum to marry Bathsheba, only to have thrust in his face at the end the newspaper account of the wedding in Bath.

[2] We shall note later the one remarkable exception of *Jude the Obscure.*

types and classes of men, an order practically extinct since the time that Mr. Hardy began to write of it, since the railways came to interrupt the continuity of tradition and break the molds. And then it is the manners and customs that have crystallized about this order, suiting themselves to these ways of maintaining life, the modes under which men and women have expressed the joy of life and found consolation for its sorrows, their style of etiquette and philosophy and humor. And finally there is the sharpness of vision by which the author has penetrated its meanings, the art with which he has composed its divers aspects, and the love with which he has brooded over all, the deep poetic sentiment by virtue of which he can hardly speak of the more signal beauties of his subject without falling into musical cadence.

Quite different in feeling are the descriptions of nature in *A Pair of Blue Eyes* and *Far from the Madding Crowd*. Mr. Hardy, in the Preface of 1895, characterizes the scene of the earlier story as "a region of dream and mystery," to which the various features of the seaside lend "an atmosphere like the twilight of a night vision." But in the book he did not succeed overwell in creating such an atmosphere. And if he had done so, it would still not satisfy the demands of our imagination nourished on the more substantial reality of his settings in later books, where the characters are so part and parcel of the landscape and product of the soil. Egdon Heath, in *The Native*, is truly enough "a region of dream and mystery," with an "atmosphere like the twilight of a night vision." And Clym, the "native," gathering furze, the reddleman camped by night in the sandpit under the hill, and the "anxious wanderers" in the rainy midnight of November, belong to this scene in a way quite different from that in which Elfride and the parson belong to the vicarage of Endelstow. In *A Pair of Blue Eyes* we have landscapes, and charming ones; we have sufficient indications of direction and the lay of the land. But we have not that sense of the fundamental topography, the underlying anatomy of the landscape, which is so prominent in *The Native*, *The Woodlanders*, and *Tess;* and which is first impressed on the reader in *Far from the Madding Crowd*.

The city-dweller knows the country by glimpses on summer afternoons when the weather is fine. It is in winter and by night, in storm and wind, that the country yields up its intimacies; then alone it reveals itself to those who actually live in its bosom, to those who must meet the elements in person, and cannot take shelter in the securities of the walled town. One cannot account for the beauty and the convincing air of nature that invests the action of Hardy's stories until one realizes how almost exclusively it takes place out of doors, and how largely by night, under black or starry skies, and with the utmost freedom of ventilation. If he would give us an impression of the life of the shepherd, he begins with the bleak hillside where his hut is perched, and the wind beating about the corners and playing its various tunes upon the trees, the grass, and the fallen leaves.

The thin grasses, more or less coating the hill, were touched by the wind in breezes of differing powers, and almost of differing natures—one rubbing the blades heavily, another raking them piercingly, another brushing them like a soft broom. The instinctive act of human kind was to stand and listen, and learn how the trees on the right and the trees on the left wailed or chaunted to each other in the regular antiphonies of a cathedral choir, how hedges and other shapes to leeward then caught the note, lowering it to the tenderest sob, and how the hurrying gust then plunged into the south, to be heard no more.

It is with senses refreshed and gratified that we accompany Gabriel Oak in his night journey to Weatherbury, reckoning the hour no more by the sun or by the hands of a clock, but by the angle of Charles's Wain to the Pole star, judging the distance of the receding wagon not by sight but by hearing, as the "crunching jangle of the waggon dies upon the ear," and informing ourselves through the soles of our feet that it is plowed land we have leaped upon, the other side of the gate. We are making across the field with Gabriel toward the great fire, which appears about half a mile away; and as we get nearer, we see his weary face "painted over with a rich orange glow, and the whole front of his smock-frock and gaiters covered with a dancing shadow pattern of thorn-twigs—the light reaching him through a leafless intervening hedge—and the metallic curve of his sheep-crook silver-bright in the same abounding rays."

Perhaps the most living scene of drama in the book is that where Gabriel and Bathsheba thatch the wheat-ricks amid the incessant flashes of the storm. The fearful crash and the sulphurous smell in the air when a tree is struck by lightning serve to impress us with the courage of Bathsheba, and make natural the emotional state in which she confides to Gabriel the circumstances of her marriage. And since we are dealing here with a man professionally weatherwise, we are privileged to read with him the complicated signs of coming storm as notified by toads and slugs and by his sheep. "Apparently there was to be a thunder-storm, and afterwards a cold continuous rain. The creeping things seemed to know all about the later rain, but little of the interpolated thunder-storm; whilst the sheep knew all about the thunder-storm and nothing of the later rain."

Such precision in the noting of natural phenomena at times and seasons strange to the dweller in towns might perhaps be cultivated deliberately by a painter of rural life determined to give to his human narrative as fresh and true an air as the notebooks of Richard Jefferies or Mr. Hudson. But only the lift of the heart, only the rhythmical pulsation of deep emotion, could give to his phrases that poetic cast—worthy of Mr. Hudson himself—which one feels in so many passages of description.

It was now early spring—the time of going to grass with the sheep, when they have the first feed of the meadows, before these are laid up for mowing. . . . . The vegetable world begins to move and swell and the saps to rise, till in the completest silence of lone gardens and trackless plantations, where everything seems helpless and still after the bond and slavery of frost. . . . .

Only the instinct to prolong the sensation of beauty could lead him into cadences so delicately turned. The phrases go in pairs as in the prose of Sir Thomas Browne or other relishers of words that balance and reinforce one another.

It is again with sentiment like that of the doctor of Norwich that the Dorchester story-teller describes "the panoramic glide of the stars past earthly objects."

The poetry of motion is a phrase much in use, and to enjoy the epic form of that gratification it is necessary to stand on a hill at a small hour of the night, and, having first expanded with a sense of difference from the mass of civilized mankind, who are horizontal and disregardful of all such proceedings at this time, long and quietly watch your stately progress through the stars. After such a nocturnal reconnoitre among these astral clusters, aloft from the customary haunts of thought and vision, some men may feel raised to a capability for eternity at once.

So stood Gabriel Oak, and told the time of night by certain starry indications. And then, because he was a man conscious of a charm in the life he led,

He stood still after looking at the sky as a useful instrument, and regarded it in an appreciative spirit, as a work of art superlatively beautiful. For a moment he seemed impressed with the speaking loneliness of the scene, or rather with the complete abstraction from all its compass of the sights and sounds of man. Human shapes, interferences, troubles, and joys were all as if they were not, and there seemed to be on the shaded hemisphere of the globe no sentient being save himself; he could fancy them all gone round to the sunny side.

Such passages occupy very little space in *Far from the Madding Crowd*, and they are seldom detachable. Readers who feel the impulse to skip them in order to get on with the story might almost as well not give their time to the reading of Hardy. For they make a difference out of all proportion to their length and prominence. They are largely what give color and fragrancy and the freshness of earth to novels which more than any others in English suggest the beauties of painting or of poetry. And they count for much in the sense of reality which one has so strong in the greater novels of Hardy. One never feels here that vagueness and thinness—that impalpability—which attaches to the place and action in so many excellent works of fiction. We know by the evidence of all our senses that we are dealing here with "substantial things."

6

But this is only the physical background of the story. There is another background of equal importance, to which much greater attention is paid by the author— the social background, made up of the numerous minor characters from the Wessex peasantry. These humble characters are almost invariably treated in a light and playful manner, and they constitute the "comic relief" in the generally somber stories. It is mainly on these rustic humors that the author relies to make palpable the old order of things, which counts for so much in making his stories lifelike as well as picturesque. It is they that furnish the rich subsoil of custom and belief in which the main action is so securely rooted. Like the deep bed of rotting leaves in an ancient forest, they give forth an acrid woodsy perfume that stirs more than anything else the sense of the successive generations of life. Over them broods the author's humor, that composite of tenderness, amusement, and reverence which plays about the moss-grown, tenacious institutions doomed in the end to yield to a new order.

Mr. Hardy had already made one charming study of such types in *The Greenwood Tree*. This is largely taken up with the quaint west-gallery fiddlers of the Mellstock choir, their round of Christmas carols, and the vain attempt to prevent their supersession by a more up-to-date organist or harmonium-player. These ancient amateurs are well satisfied of their own competence, and they cannot find words strong enough to express their abhorrence of the intrusive new instruments. They know what is seemly in the service of the Lord; and they are deeply shocked when, for the first time in the history of the church, the singing from the girls' side takes on a fulness and independence as great as that of the choir itself. Heretofore "the girls, like the rest of the congregation, had always been humble and respectful followers of the gallery, singing at sixes and sevens if without gallery leaders, never interfering with the ordinances of these practiced artists—having no will, union, power, or proclivity except it was given them from the established choir enthroned above them." As one of the gallery puts it, " 'Tis the gallery have got to sing, all the world knows." But now they have received clear notice of their obsoleteness.

It is natural that the converse of such people should be largely of a reminiscential sort, like that of Justice Shallow, and full of anecdotes retailed with full Shakespearean gusto. Slight experiences of a humorous or surprising nature are treasured with all the fondness of men whose lives are not rich in excitement or variety; and friends never tire of hearing how Tranter Dewy was taken in in the purchase of a cider cask, or how the shoemaker once identified a drowned man by the mere sight of the family foot.

The social obscurity of these people does not prevent them from showing a decided proficiency in the art of conversation, which means even more to them than to people with greater resources for amusement. The author often calls attention to the instinct with which they determine how far to carry a given topic, as where the shoemaker, who had been showing his last, "seemed to perceive that the sum-total of interest the object had excited was greater than he had anticipated, and warranted the last's being taken up again and exhibited." And what is lacking in the actual substance of the words spoken is amply made up in the range and subtlety of tone, gesture, facial expression, all noted by the author with loving care. The taking in of Tranter Dewy by a sharp salesman is occasion for a great variety of vocal expression.

"Ah, who can believe sellers!" said old Michael Mail in a *carefully-cautious voice*, by way of tiding-over this critical point of affairs.

"No one at all," said Joseph Bowman, in *the tone of a man fully agreeing with everybody*.

"Ay," said Mail, in *the tone of a man who did not agree with everybody as a rule, though he did now;* "I know'd a auctioneering fellow once. . . . ."[1]

and so on to an anecdote.

All the resources of manner are drawn upon by these simple people in the interest of decency, politeness, and mutual consideration. They have learned very well how to subordinate the mere appetites of the body to the more elegant demands of social intercourse. While Mr. Penny was explaining the interesting points of a certain last, "his left hand wandered towards the cider-cup, as if the hand had no connection with the person speaking." He felt that one need not call attention crudely to the act of refreshing the inner man. When Mrs. Dewy at the Christmas party mentioned the subject of supper, "that portion of the company

[1] P. 14.

who loved eating and drinking put on a look to signify that till that moment they had quite forgotten that it was customary to expect suppers on these occasions; going even further than this politeness of feature, and starting irrelevant subjects, the exceeding flatness and forced tone of which rather betrayed their object." Delicate subjects are carefully avoided by these peaceable and sensitive natures, and there is always someone ready with a remark like Michael Mail, in "a carefully cautious voice, by way of tiding-over" any "critical point of affairs." When Mrs. Dewy mentions the awkward circumstance that "Reuben always was such a hot man," Mr. Penny knows how to imply "the correct species of sympathy that such an affliction required, by trying to smile and to look grieved at the same time." Mr. Dewy is the mildest and most full of resources for social conciliation of anyone in Mellstock parish. When he, as leader of the delegation to the vicar, wishes to broach the ticklish subject of the church music, "what I have been thinking," he says, and implies "by this use of the past tense that he was hardly so discourteous as to be positively thinking it then."

Nothing speaks more eloquently of the delicacy and good-nature of these simple folk than their attitude toward Thomas Leaf, the parish fool. Leaf made frequent candid acknowledgment of the fact that he "never had no head"; and "they all assented to this, not with any sense of humiliating Leaf by disparaging him after an open confession, but because it was an accepted thing that Leaf didn't in the least mind having no head, that deficiency of his being an unimpassioned matter of parish history." And since his family was in general the most melancholy in their experience, and since Leaf sang a very high treble and they didn't know "what they should do without en for upper G," they consented, on the tranter's motion, to let him come along with them to the famous interview with Parson Maybold. On that occasion he was treated by everyone with the same tender consideration, and the same combination of pity and of satisfaction taken in his peculiar defect. Quite similar was the treatment of other fools in later novels—of the bashful Joseph Poorgrass in *The Madding Crowd*, and the half-witted Christian Cantle in *The Native*. By virtue of its humaneness, the community spirit managed to turn a social liability into a social asset.

It is on the whole a very attractive picture of Wessex humanity that Mr. Hardy gives us in these rustic sketches: meekly submissive to what they take for the decrees of fate, backward and without initiative, naïve, and of limited vision; but mild and innocent, abounding in social refinements, and full of the milk of human kindness. It is a picture bearing the stamp of truth, and done with great delicacy and sympathetic feeling, in a manner suggesting that of Addison, of Goldsmith, or of Shakespeare.

7

The rustic humors were practically the whole subject of this "rural painting of the Dutch school," hero and heroine being so much less substantial figures than those of the "background" itself. The background figures themselves were not deeply conceived; and there was no such opportunity as in *The Madding Crowd* to use them for deepening the harmonies of a richer orchestration.

In *The Madding Crowd* there is a serious main plot, in connection with which the rustic humors find their significant employment. They make a true chorus to the doings of the great ones, applying to an action outside their own scope and capacity the general social philosophy in relation to which it must be viewed. They make up the audience before whom Bathsheba Everdene plays her part. They are also actually made use of in carrying forward the story. It is in conversations among them that many circumstances of the action transpire. In one case they are made the unconscious instruments in provoking the central catastrophe. For it was Joseph Poorgrass' love of comfort and the cup that delayed the arrival of Fanny's coffin so that it was determined to leave it for the night in Bathsheba's sitting-room. He is thus as great an instrument of tragedy as Christian Cantle in *The Return of the Native*, whose indulgence in the folly of the dice box results in such fatal bitterness and misunderstanding.

Hardy had up to this time produced no humorous passage so rich in ironic overtones as this scene in the Buck's Head Inn, where Joseph, intrusted with the transference of Fanny's body from the Casterbridge poorhouse to Weatherbury church, takes comfort in a mug of ale with his pals, while the flower-laden coffin waits in the rain. It was but solemn conviviality in which they indulged, displaying their wisdom chiefly on the subject of religion. But the judgment of Gabriel is none the less severe, when he finds his messenger drunk in the company of drunkards, because he "does

his wicked deeds in such confoundedly holy ways."
However, the topers are by now too well armed against
all ills to be much troubled by Gabriel's reproaches.
Mark Clark expresses his convivial philosophy in a song
celebrating the advantage of today over tomorrow as a
time for feasting. And Jan Coggan, more profound,
more cynical, and more to the point, makes their
measured defense, speaking, toper-like, "with the
precision of a machine."

"Nobody can hurt a dead woman. All that could be done for
her is done—she's beyond us: and why should a man put himself
in a tearing hurry for lifeless clay that can neither feel nor see,
and don't know what you do with her at all? If she'd been alive,
I would have been the first to help her. If she now wanted
victuals and drink, I'd pay for it, money down. But she's dead
and no speed of ours will bring her back to life. . . . . Drink,
shepherd, and be friends, for tomorrow we may be like her."

But we are not left with a drunkard's view of the
matter. Gabriel and Bathsheba are tender enough in
their concern for even the lifeless body of Fanny; and
the parson at least knows how to take his cue. "Perhaps
Mrs. Troy is right in feeling that we cannot treat a dead
fellow-creature too thoughtfully. We must remember
that though she may have erred grievously in leaving
her home, she is still our sister; and it is to be believed
that God's uncovenanted mercies are extended towards
her, and that she is a member of the flock of Christ."
"The parson's words spread out into the heavy air
with a sad yet unperturbed cadence." It is just such
a cadence that the rustics have generally a perfect
command of. Especially the topers of the Buck's Head
have the whole range of sanctimonious expression, and

know how to use a pious tone in reference to their own frailties. Even their capacity for liquor "is a talent the Lord has mercifully bestowed upon us, and we ought not to neglect it."

Hardy, like a true humorist, knows how to give us, by infinite fine touches, a sense of the droll puppet-like speech and movement of the humble upon earth, copies as they are of the great ones, but sufficiently reduced in stature so that we, the great ones, may laugh at them without too vivid a consciousness of kinship. They are, however, but copies of their masters, with the same aspirations and pretensions, caught in the same machinery of circumstance, enveloped by the same atmosphere of dim brightness in the midst of a wide obscurity. It is a characteristic feature in the Wessex composition that the denizens of these secluded valleys should discuss with simple wonder the ways of "strange cities"—how, in Bath, for a present example, the people "never need to light their fires except as a luxury, for the water springs up out of the earth ready boiled for use." It is pleasantly characteristic of more than Wessex humanity, the way Joseph Poorgrass comes to the defense of his simple-minded friend for some rather incoherent statement with his own naïve philosophical reflections: "Let en alone. The boy's maning that the sky and the earth in the kingdom of Bath is not altogether different from ours here. 'Tis for our good to gain knowledge of strange cities, and as such the boy's words should be suffered, so to speak it."

Not the least happy trait of human nature, in its littleness and imperfection, is the disposition to take a complacent view of one's circumstances, even when they reflect no particular credit upon one, and especially to make the most of one's defects. The blushful timidity of Joseph Poorgrass arouses so much interest in the countrymen gathered at Warren's malthouse that it comes to fill him "with a mild complacency." Later we find him actually regarding his extreme modesty in the presence of women as a sort of superior gift to which he was born, and an occasion for hiding his light—rather ostentatiously—under a bushel. It may be that the point is a bit labored for effect. Certainly more delicious in its humorous truthfulness is the maltster's childish pride in his extreme old age—that being the most remarkable fact about him. It is his son Jacob— himself a man of the considerable age of sixty-five, who, to put his father in good humor, suggests that he should favor the newly arrived shepherd with "the pedigree of his life." This the maltster proceeds to do, after clearing his throat and elongating his gaze, "in the slow speech justifiable when the importance of a subject is so generally felt that any mannerism must be tolerated." After he has given the items of his career—how long he lived in each of the places where he has labored—another old gentleman "given to mental arithmetic" calculates the number of years as one hundred and seventeen.

"Well, then, that's my age," said the maltster, emphatically.

"Oh, no, father!" said Jacob. "Your turnip-hoeing were in the summer and your malting in the winter of the same years, and ye don't ought to count both halves, father."

"Chok' it all! I lived through the summer, didn't I? That's my question. I suppose ye'll say next I be no age at all to speak of?"

"Sure we shan't," said Gabriel, soothingly.

"Ye be a very old aged person, malter," attested Jan Coggan, also soothingly. "We all know that, and ye must have a wonderful talented constitution to be able to live so long, mustn't he, neighbours?"

"True, true, ye must, malter, wonderful," said the meeting unanimously.

The maltster, being now pacified, was even generous enough to voluntarily disparage in a slight degree the virtue of having lived a great many years, by mentioning that the cup they were drinking out of was three years older than he.[1]

The same polite consideration that is shown toward Joseph and the maltster appears in the attitude of all the rustics toward one another. It implies the self-respect and the respect for one's fellow-mortal exhibited by the more heroic characters. It implies a regard for the human soul itself irrespective of social position, material possessions, intellectual attainments, and such-like irrelevant circumstances which, if we are to believe our Wordsworth and our Hardy, characterize English humanity

> Far from the madding crowd's ignoble strife.

The very farm hands approach one another with a high and simple dignity worthy of patriarchs and shepherd-kings "in the early ages of the world."

8

This spiritual culture and philosophy have their roots, we realize, in an old and well-established tradition. These humble folk are deeply conscious of a historical background. The frequenters of Warren's malthouse are well acquainted with the antecedents of their patroness of Weatherbury Farm, and can give you anecdotes from her father's domestic life. When Gabriel Oak drops in for a chat, the aged maltster can swear that he recognized by his looks the grandson of

[1] Pp. 72-73.

"Gabriel Oak over at Norcombe"; and when the new shepherd shows himself politely disregardful of a little "clean dirt" in meat and drink, it is seen that "he's his grandfer's own grandson—his grandfer were just such a nice unparticular man!"

By such means the entire picture is given that mellow consistency which we prize so highly in certain of the old masters—not that caused by the fading and toning down of colors, but that which comes of a sentiment for objects harmonized themselves by the composing brush of time. The architectural backgrounds are always such as to make us feel the age and ripeness of this society. The author dwells with tender awe upon the long use and the nobility of design of the great shearing-barn, resembling a church in its ground plan, "wealthy in material," with its "dusky, filmed, chestnut roof, braced and tied in by huge collars, curves, and diagonals." It was four centuries old. "Standing before this abraded pile, the eye regarded its present usage, the mind dwelt upon its past history, with a satisfied sense of functional continuity throughout—a feeling almost of gratitude, and quite of pride, at the permanence of the idea which had heaped it up."

Hardy has studied well the less sublime among the Dutch masters, and his own pictures have often a suggestion of the manner of Terburg or Gerard Douw. But still more one is reminded, by interiors and night scenes out of doors, in *The Native* and *The Madding Crowd*, of the deep and eloquent chiaroscuro of Rembrandt. Hardy loves to note the effects of a small point of bright light, with its rays soon dissipated in the surrounding gloom. He loves to show the gigantic shadows of human figures about a fire, or the "wheeling rays" from a passing lantern cast on the ceiling of a room. The old men were sitting about in the dark corners of the malthouse. The room "was lighted only by the ruddy glow from the kiln mouth, which shone over the floor with the streaming horizontality of the setting sun, and threw upward the shadows of all facial irregularities in those assembled round." Out of the prevailing darkness would come the slow, deliberate accents of the speakers, as half-guessed incidents of ancient history emerge from the soundless obscurity of lost ages. The topers of the Buck's Head were sinking into the double dimness of the misty day and the evening twilight, symbolic of human weakness and ignorance. As the comfort of the strong drink stole over them, their consciousness of mortal sorrows and obligations itself grew dim. "The longer Joseph Poorgrass remained, the less his spirit was troubled by the duties which devolved upon him this afternoon. The minutes glided by uncounted, until the evening shades began perceptibly to deepen, and the eyes of the three were but sparkling points on the surface of darkness."

Such scenes and the sentiment associated with them give to the whole composition a depth of imaginative appeal which would not derive from the main action taken by itself. It is the depth of poetic feeling, the depth we recognize as that of life itself. All is in perfect keeping. And so by the magic of harmonic enrichment, the story of *Far from the Madding Crowd* takes on a degree of truth and beauty which for the first time we are willing to acknowledge as entirely worthy of the genius of Thomas Hardy.

IV. DRAMA

In *Far from the Madding Crowd*, it was the setting which we had to thank for the comparative shapeliness of the work.   In *The Return of the Native*, we have an actual principle of form, organic and compelling.   It is what we may call the dramatic idea.   This is the first of the novels of Hardy to exhibit in striking fashion that tendency to dramatic structure which is so generally prominent in the novels of today, and which has been coming into fashion since about the time of its conception.

I

The Return of the Native is a tragedy of irreconcilable ideals.   For most readers the main character will be Eustacia Vye, a woman of rich and stormy passions, pent up in a lonely place, and longing for the larger and livelier movement of the great world.   The great world is symbolized to her by the animated watering-place only a few hours' drive from her home on Egdon Heath; and then, as her horizon broadens, by the elegance and luxury of Paris.   But while she longs for Paris, type of elegance and luxury, the native of Egdon Heath is returning from that center of the world, tired of its vanity and frivolous worldliness, to plain living and high thinking in the desert.   And so the destinies have spun the web which is to entangle the strong hearts of Clym Yeobright and Eustacia Vye.

Already Eustacia has experienced the passion of love, yielding herself to the wooing of Mr. Wildeve, the gentlemanly innkeeper, whom she has met in the lonely places of the heath beneath Rainbarrow. Wildeve, on his part, has gone so far with another woman as to jeopardize her good name. This is Thomasin Yeobright, a cousin of Clym's, whom Wildeve promised to marry, but left in the lurch. Wildeve and Eustacia are ruthless players of the game of love, drawn together and repelled according to the pagan laws of jealousy, vanity, and pique. But swiftly she recognizes the better man on his appearance; and swiftly the latter yields to the immortal fascination. It is the plan of Clym to give up the world, and trade, and wealth, to settle upon the lonely heath, his home, and to make himself a teacher of the natives—leading them in the simple ways of the spirit. This is quite contrary to Eustacia's notion of a liberal life; but she believes that in the long run she can win him over to her views. Accordingly she provokes Wildeve to carry out his promise of marriage to Thomasin, and she herself marries the man from Paris.

But it is the man's will that prevails. They go to live in a cottage on the heath while Clym is preparing himself for his mission. And then, when his eyes give out from overstudy, and he goes forth to work alone as furze-cutter, clad all in leather and scarcely human to the eye, she has to watch him turning back to the peasant's estate and not unhappy in this occasion to demonstrate his Tolstoian philosophy. Meantime Wildeve has been made independent of the narrow life by receiving a legacy; and it is he who comes to represent for her the world of freedom and expansiveness.

The tragedy is brought to its climax by misunderstanding with Clym's mother. Mrs. Yeobright had always been opposed to the marriage with Eustacia, whom she regards as a "bad woman"; and it is long after their wedding before she can make up her mind to visit them. And by an evil chance—involving the presence of Wildeve with Eustacia—she is turned away from their closed door to plod disconsolate across the heath, and—again by an evil chance—to meet her death. And so arise misunderstanding, suspicion, and black words between Clym and Eustacia, and they go to live apart, each in his own home. They are both in despair; and through a combination of chance and voluntary action, Eustacia sets out on a dark and rainy night to join Wildeve and go with him to a brighter world. But in the end she cannot bring herself to such an act of perfidy—Wildeve is not "great enough for her desire." And seeing no way out, she leaps into the black pool of the millrace. She is followed by Wildeve and Clym; and when the three bodies are dragged out at last, it is only Clym in whom the breath of life remains. He is left, a bruised and crippled soul, to preach the gospel of the simple life. Eustacia, for whom his gospel was but empty words, stifled and starved on Egdon Heath, could find no outlet in life for her abounding and rebellious energy.

I take no account of the after-lives of Thomasin and her faithful lover Diggory Venn, since these seem not to have been included in the author's original plan of the tragic story. Thomasin and Diggory are, like Mrs. Yeobright and Wildeve himself, but counters in the great game in which the players are Clym and Eustacia. Their game it is which gives to this novel its structural likeness to a play.

2

What distinguishes a play from a novel is its brevity and its confinement to dialogue as means of telling the story. Owing to these restrictions the writer of plays is forced to certain economies which the novelist does not have to consider. Many entertaining features, many means of developing his subject, he is obliged to eliminate for the sake of concentration, in order to get his effect in the short space of time allowed and in the form of dialogue. And this very concentration, this very elimination of features not directly subservient to his effect, result in a certain simplicity of form which is hailed by the critical taste as one of the chief beauties of the drama.

English playwrights have not always acknowledged the limitations of the genre. The drama of Shakespeare is largely a superb and impudent denial of this dramatic idea. But, with less power and weaker imagination, we have returned in modern times to a stricter observance of the dramatic laws. The theory of Dryden is much more in harmony than the practice of Shakespeare with the conception of the play which prevailed equally in the times of Euripides, of Racine, of Ibsen and Dumas, of Schnitzler and Galsworthy.

The essence of drama as conceived in our own times is the presentation of a single situation in which a set of characters find themselves related to one another by alliance or opposition according to their attitude toward some issue, some point in dispute. The alignment changes from act to act as one phase or another of the issue comes to the fore, as one point or another is determined. There are infinite shifts in the balance of power, as intrigue and diplomacy detach certain parties from their neutrality or cause a belligerent to change sides. But the major parties to the controversy generally hold the stage without interruption; and the changing action continues throughout to be a tug of war between the major parties. Drama is a matter of tensions, and the strength of each act is in proportion to the intensity of pull between the antagonists.

The dramatic principle requires accordingly close continuity of action, in order that momentum may not be lost. The pull must be continuous throughout the act; so that, in this interest, act and scene (in the English sense of the word) are identical.

And no act stands alone. The strength of one act depends upon the degree of interest held over from that which goes before. The brevity of the play allows of little in the way of new incident, new persons, new issues, which would require a certain amount of exposition and so relax the tension. Each act takes up the situation at a stage directly following that of the one before, with the balance of power arrived at in the climax of the earlier act, in order to move forward to a new climax and a new balance of power.

One situation, one issue throughout the piece. It is conceivable that a play so built might have no general theme, no social thesis or idea. It might conceivably present an adventure, the pursuit of crown or lady, in which the issue waited upon the outcome of many diplomatic moves, upon the crossing of intellectual swords in the seclusion of cabinet or publicity of cabaret. It might be of the stuff of Dumas *père*, of Anthony Hope, handled with the technique of Ibsen or Dumas *fils*. But in point of fact, the drama of a single issue proves to be the drama of a single theme, the *pièce à thèse*. It is *The Master Builder, Le Demimonde, Der Einsame Weg, Justice, The Playboy of the Western World*. It is the theme which *defines* the situation, which determines the roster of characters, which eliminates unnecessary incident, which binds together act to act, and maintains suspense at a white heat.

And so it comes about that the drama, strictly defined, is a highly subjective product. What happens is subordinate to what is felt. This is evident from Aeschylus to Racine, from Dryden and Marivaux to Ibsen and Maeterlinck. It is not merely conventional "decency" which relegates bloodshed to behind-the-scenes or to the narrative of servant or messenger. It is the sense of the comparative irrelevancy of objective incident, preoccupation with that moral struggle which makes the drama. What happens is reduced to a minimum; and attention is concentrated upon the subjective accompaniment of action and incident. Whatever happens or is done releases accordingly an enormously greater volume of psychological energy than what happens or is done in an adventure story—in Anthony Hope or Dumas père.

And the pattern of the plot becomes so simple that lovers of intrigue and spectacle cry out against its monotony. But the lovers of drama cherish it for its neatness and finish. They find a charm in features which were adopted for their utility. The unities, which were invented as means toward dramatic concentration, become an end in themselves; like courage or fidelity,

virtues cherished by the race for their survival value—
for their mere utility—which have become as lovely as
roses and lilies in our eyes, to be cultivated for themselves by all who love beauty.

3

To a large degree, the cultivation of form in the novel
is the cultivation, consciously or not, of the dramatic
idea. In the time of Fielding and Smollett, when the
novel was the foster-child of rambling chronicles,
Don Quixote and *Gil Blas;* in the time of Thackeray
and Dickens, their followers, when there was no drama
in England—the novel was purely a narrative of adventures, or a parade of droll and picturesque characters.
The very antipodes of the dramatic idea may be found
in *The Adventures of Roderick Random* or in *The Personal
History of David Copperfield*.

In *David Copperfield*, nearly a third of the book is
through before one runs upon any hint of a plot.
Nowhere can one distinguish a theme of any kind—even
an issue—even a situation in which one becomes conscious of dramatic tensions. David and Agnes drift
along in a slow-moving current, in a barque in which
the only ones who pull at an oar are Mr. Micawber and
Uriah Heep. The only excitement of the book is aroused
over the fate of Little Em'ly—I will not say her story,
for her story is never told. We are never given her
version of her love affair—never made to feel what she
suffered, how she was tempted, how she was brought
to her fateful act, or on what terms she lived with the
man who is supposed to have exerted the fatal fascination. In her story, in the story of Dr. Strong and his

young wife, in the story of Miss Trotwood and her good-for-nothing husband, and in the story of David and Dora, there were the materials of drama, of "problem," of social thesis. It seems as if the Victorian author, unhappily married himself, were vaguely anticipating the sort of study in marital infelicity which was going to be made so abundantly in a later generation. But he never raises, in the case of any of these, a real dramatic issue; he confines himself to the droll and pathetic aspects of speech and incident. He takes every possible occasion to divert our attention from the main characters to minor and intrusive figures, from the main action—if such can be discovered—to the infinite petty happenings that lead from nowhere to nowhere, unless it be from the cradle to the grave. It is a moving picture without plot and without subject. It is true the pictures are very fine. But there is nothing in common between the moving picture and the drama.

Before Dickens there had been many English novels, and there were many in his time, in which a limited subject and a neatly defined plot make for the shapeliness and concentration of a well-made play. It is often so in Walter Scott, and invariably so in Jane Austen. A close-joined conflict over a well-defined issue sometimes gives to a novel of Trollope's, like *Barchester Towers*, a dramatic effectiveness seldom reached by Dickens. The evidence of careful design is everywhere present in the work of George Eliot, appearing, for one thing, in her most frequent division of the story into books. It is clear that she has thought out with philosophical precision all the bearings of her theme, and chosen her characters with reference to it. In a book like *Adam Bede*, the number of the characters and the period covered are carefully limited; and the action proceeds in a straight line and with accelerating force from start to finish.

But, apart from this work of Hardy, the first important novel of the Victorian period in which the author was strongly and consciously under the control of the dramatic idea was perhaps *The Egoist*, published in 1879, the year following *The Return of the Native*. It was in 1877 that Meredith delivered his famous lecture on comedy; and while he was using the word in a broad sense to cover various forms employed by the comic spirit, it was the comic play—it was Menander, Molière, and the English comedy of manners—which mainly held his attention. And it was obviously under the influence of the comic stage that he designed and wrote the history of the engagement of Sir Willoughby Patterne. His idea was to give a comic exhibition of egoism as it was brought into play in this crucial love affair. The place and time and extent of the action were all reduced to the smallest possible compass in order that the section of human nature observed might be brought under a glass of the highest magnifying power. The scene is practically limited to Patterne Hall, during the few weeks of a summer visit of the Middletons; and the action has to do altogether with the efforts of Clara to get released from her engagement and Sir Willoughby's desperate efforts to keep his social prestige unimpaired. There is no presentation of the early life of Sir Willoughby, of his antecedent love affairs, or even of his courtship. Within the limits of the story nothing happens of greater objective magnitude than Clara's abortive flight to the railway station, her horseback ride with De Craye, and Crossjay's eaves-dropping at Sir Willoughby's proposal to Laetitia Dale. The substance of the story is made up of diplomatic *pourparlers*, dinner-party fencing, and the long-drawn, carefully masked struggle of Sir Willoughby not to become the object of public ridicule and commiseration: a struggle—this being very "high" comedy—which results in the equivocal triumph of his engagement to Laetitia. For the reader who finds himself really concerned in the feelings of the characters, as repre-sentative mortals, a great and steadily growing suspense attaches to this action, in spite of the small provision of objective incident, or perhaps rather because of this small provision. The reader's interest is like an electric current running to heat in a slender thread of metal, and grows more and more intense, even to the point of incandescence, for the very reason that there is so little in the way of objective incident upon which it may discharge itself.

Since the time of Meredith this fashion of story-telling has taken enormously. The most notable instances of stories built upon this plan are the novels of James, especially those following *The Spoils of Poynton*, such as *The Awkward Age* and *The Ambassadors*, in which the relation is very clear between the formal neatness and the predominance of a single theme. More recently the style is very much in evidence, if not positively in the ascendant, as one may see by a review of the work of Mr. George Moore and Mr. Galsworthy, of Mrs. Wharton and Mr. Walpole, of Mr. Hergesheimer and

Miss Sinclair. Consider simply the titles of Mr. Galsworthy: *Fraternity, The Country House, The Man of Property, The Patrician;* or of Mrs. Wharton: *The House of Mirth, The Age of Innocence.*

4

In his early novels we might say that Mr. Hardy was treating a subject, but not a theme. In *Far from the Madding Crowd*, for instance, he took up the subject of Wessex country life; and his characters and plot were so chosen as to introduce the typical incidents in the business of shepherd and farmer. It is these incidents that stand out most prominently, and make the most vivid appeal to the reader's imagination. And then, as the borrowed plot asserts itself, it is the melodramatic incidents necessary to its development that make the main impression—Troy's outburst over the coffin of Fanny and the shooting of Troy at Boldwood's Christmas party. We are interested indeed in the fortunes and happiness of Bathsheba; but there is no clear dramatic issue, nothing around which can gather our interest in her mental experience. The best the author can do is to make her actions seem plausible; and sometimes we have a feeling that the incidents are rather forced to fit the arbitrary pattern of the plot.

But with *The Return of the Native*, Hardy has taken up a theme which involves a clear-cut issue in the minds of the leading characters, and especially in the mind of Eustacia, which is the main stage of the drama. It is her stifled longing for spiritual expansion which leads her to play with the love of Wildeve, which causes her later to throw him over for the greater promise of

Clym, which leads her back again to Wildeve, and at last—with the loss of all hope—to suicide. In every case it requires but the smallest outlay of incident to provoke the most lively play of feeling; and the play of feeling—the opposition of desires—is embodied here, in true dramatic fashion, in talk rather than in acts. It takes nothing more than the return of Thomasin from town unwed to set going the whole series of dialogues which make up the substance of the first book, dialogues in which Wildeve and Mrs. Yeobright, Venn and Eustacia, Eustacia and Wildeve do nothing more than fence with one another, each maneuvering for position in a breathless game of well-matched antagonists. These are scenes in the true dramatic sense, not in the popular sense that calls for violence and surprising action.

In the third book the main thing that happens is a quarrel between Clym and his mother over Eustacia. The wedding itself is not presented, having no dramatic value. The dramatic value of the book is indicated in its caption, "The Fascination," the drama lying in the resistless attraction to one another of two persons so far apart in mind.

In the fourth book we have the major incident of Mrs. Yeobright's death on the day when she was turned away from Eustacia's door. But there is none of the bustle of action about this narrative; and, especially at the end, it is the *feeling*, the pathos, the spiritual significance, of the events that is rendered. There is one scene of special impressiveness. It consists in the talk between Mrs. Yeobright, as she plods wearily homeward across the heath on a stifling August day, and little Johnny Nunsuch trotting beside her and plying her with the cruel, naïve questions of a child. This is all done in the weird, intense manner of symbolistic drama—something of Ibsen or Maeterlinck—in which the characters are children and old women, gifted with preternatural vision. Objective facts are but as objects seen in some magic crystal, whereof the meaning is mystic, and deeper than material reality. In her state of supreme spiritual prostration, the old woman goes forward with introverted eyes, replying candidly, and with a kind of gratefulness for his simplicity which enables her to unbosom her sorrow, to the simple, searching questions of the little boy.

> Mrs. Yeobright spoke to him as one in a mesmeric sleep.
> " 'Tis a long way home, my child, and we shall not get there till evening."
> "I shall," said her small companion. "I am going to play marnels afore supper, and we go to supper at six o'clock, because father comes home. Does your father come home at six too?"
> "No: he never comes; nor my son either, nor anybody."
> "What have made you so down? Have you seen a ooser?"
> "I have seen what's worse—a woman's face looking at me through a window-pane."[1]

As Mrs. Yeobright goes on talking to herself, raging against the cruelty of Eustacia and Clym, Johnny remarks:

> "You must be a very curious woman to talk like that."
> "O no, not at all," she said, returning to the boy's prattle. "Most people who grow up and have children talk as I do. When you grow up your mother will talk as I do."
> "I hope she won't; because 'tis very bad to talk nonsense."
> "Yes, child; it is nonsense, I suppose. Are you not nearly spent with the heat?"

[1] P. 355.

"Yes, but not so much as you be."

"How do you know?"

"Your face is white and wet, and your head is hanging-down-like."

"Ah, I am exhausted from inside."

"Why do you, every time you take a step, go like this?" The child in speaking gave to his motion the jerk and limp of an invalid.

"Because I have a burden which is more than I can bear."[1]

And then when she has seated herself to rest,

"How funny you draw your breath"—says Johnny— "like a lamb when you drive him till he's nearly done for. Do you always draw your breath like that?"

"Not always." Her voice was so low as to be scarcely above a whisper.

"You will go to sleep there, I suppose, won't you? You have shut your eyes already."

"No, I shall not sleep much till—another day, and then I hope to have a long, long one—very long."[2]

There are few places in which Hardy—few places in which any English novelist—has made himself so completely free from the commonplace bustle of the theater, and has made us hear so pure and unstrained the voices of the inner drama.

5

Never before in Hardy had the machinery of action been so masked and subordinated. Never again perhaps was it to occupy a place of so little prominence in his work. It is only once or twice in Meredith, and more generally in the later novels of James, that we find so great a volume of emotional energy released by events of so little objective importance. Only in them is found a greater economy of incident; and many more readers

[1] Pp. 355–56.   [2] P. 356.

will testify to the dramatic intensity of *The Native* than to that of *The Egoist* or *The Golden Bowl*.

The whole course of the story was conceived by the author in terms suggestive of physics and dynamics. Each step in the plot represents the balance and reaction of forces expressible almost in algebraic formulas. Many readers have been impressed with the strong scientific coloring of Hardy's mind: with his tendency to view both external nature and the human heart with the sharpness and hard precision of a naturalist, and to record the phenomena observed with some of the abstractness of the summarizing philosopher.

Nowhere was this latter tendency exhibited in more striking fashion than in the brief arguments or abstracts prefixed to the several books in the original magazine version of *The Native*. The first book, we read, "depicts the scenes which result from *an antagonism between the hopes of four persons. . . . . By* reason of this strife of wishes, a happy consummation to all concerned is impossible, as matters stand; but *an easing of the situation* is begun by *the inevitable decadence of a too capricious love*, and rumours of a new arrival." In the second book, the stranger's arrival, "by *giving a new bias to emotions* in one quarter, *precipitates affairs* in another with unexpected rapidity." In the next book, Clym's passion for Eustacia "hampers his plans, and *causes a sharp divergence of opinion, committing him to an irretrievable step*." In the fourth book we read how "the old affection between mother and son reasserts itself"; how "a critical juncture ensues, truly the *turning point* in the lives of all concerned—*Eustacia has the move*, and she makes it; but not till the sun has set does she suspect the *consequences involved in her choice of courses.*" In the argument of the fifth book are briefly listed "*the natural effects* of the foregoing misadventures."

In these abstract statements of the action is suggested how the situation is made up of a succession of tensions, gradually tightening and relaxing, and how steady and continuous is the pull, throughout each book taken by itself, and through the history as a whole. The story as a whole is a continuous record of Eustacia's vain attempt to escape the limitations of Egdon through the means of love; and this is the key to all her tug-of-war with Wildeve and with Clym. In the first book the particular pull is between Eustacia on the one hand and Thomasin and her friends on the other, with Wildeve for the bone of contention. It becomes more and more intense to the point of Eustacia's triumph, and then lets up with her growing sense of Wildeve's mediocrity. The second book shows us Eustacia drawn to Clym, and Wildeve consequently repelled in the direction of Thomasin. The third book is wholly taken up with the fascination of Clym and the resulting disagreement and break with his mother. The fourth book records the growth of misunderstanding between man and wife on the one side, between son and mother on the other, with the resultant tragedy. The fifth book carries the strain between Clym and Eustacia to the breaking-point, and shows us Eustacia driven by Clym and drawn by Wildeve to her death.

How far we have left behind the old crude contrivance for working up excitement and suspense, that arrangement of mechanical traps for embroiling the action, that

timing of fuses for explosion at regular intervals, which is
the business of our ordinary purveyor of farce and melodrama, a business in which Mr. Hardy was himself
so often engaged! How largely he has dispensed in
The Native with such artificial aids to interest! Instead
of a set of mysteries to be solved, we are confronted at
the start with "an antagonism between the hopes of
four persons." Instead of being a series of accidents
and misunderstandings setting the characters at odds
and creating suspense as to how it will all *come out*,
the story moves forward to "sharp divergences of
opinion," and works itself out in "irretrievable steps"
and "moves" and "consequences." So it is we are
invited to observe the simple play of opposing wills,
in a situation naturally arising, with naked psychological
forces pitted against each other as directly and fairly,
with as ingenious a balance of power, as in a game of
chess.

6

The philosophical arguments to the several parts
were not retained when the story was published in book
form; but in their place the author has supplied the more
artistic and not less pregnant headings or titles, which
so aptly describe the subject-matter of the several
"books." The division of a novel into parts is always
a significant indication of an author's interest in the
logical massing of his material, in the larger architectonics
of his work. It is very little used by novelists like
Dickens; very much used by novelists like George
Eliot, Victor Hugo, Henry James, and—in our own
time—Mr. Walpole. It generally implies a bias for the
"dramatic," in so far as it involves the grouping of the

subject-matter around certain characters or great moments in the action, as that of a play is grouped in the
several acts. In *The Native* this is especially notable.
The first book is entitled "The Three Women," which
characterizes the single situation involving on the one
hand Eustacia and on the other Thomasin and Mrs.
Yeobright. The second book is "The Arrival," signalizing the new dramatic alignment caused by the first
appearance of the hero. "The Fascination" vividly
describes the following situation between Eustacia and
Clym as viewed by Mrs. Yeobright. "The Closed
Door" is the terse dramatic label for the combination
of events which issued in the death of Mrs. Yeobright.
And "The Discovery" is the slightly less effective
word for the climax between Clym and Eustacia, leading
to the tragic dénouement.

These five books are like the five acts of a classic
play. And in each book the scenes are largely grouped
around certain points in time so as to suggest the classic
continuity within the several acts. In the first book,
for example, all the scenes take place on the fifth and
sixth of November and closely follow upon the Guy
Fawkes celebration. In the second book the scenes lead
up to and center about the Christmas mumming where
first the hero and heroine "stand face to face." The
fourth book centers about, and half the scenes take place
upon, the thirty-first of August, the day of the "closed
door" and Mrs. Yeobright's death.

The whole action of the story is confined to a year
and a day, a very short period for an English novel;
and thus observes with considerable strictness what we
may call the novelistic unity of time. This was not

so much a matter of course with Hardy and his contemporaries as it is with present-day writers like
Mr. Swinnerton (*September*, *Nocturne*), Mrs. Wharton
(*Summer*), Miss Sidgwick (*Hatchways*), Mr. Marshall
(*Exton Manor*), Mr. Hergesheimer (*Java Head, Cytherea*).
It is to be accomplished only through the choice
of a plot which does admit of being compressed
within narrow limits of time. And it furthermore
requires that this plot shall be taken at its climax, and
that no attempt shall be made to present the antecedent
action save by retrospect, in the way of dialogue or
brief summary made naturally in the course of the
action presented. This is the method of Sophocles, of
Racine, or Ibsen; and if it has come to be a favorite
method with novelists like Henry James and Edith
Wharton, it is probably the drama chiefly which has
shown them the way to such a grace of form.[1] *The
Return of the Native*, first published in 1878, one year
before *The Egoist* and more than twenty years before
The Awkward Age and *The Ambassadors*, was really,
among English novels of its time, a pioneer in this
technique.

7

As for the novelistic unity of place, *The Return of
the Native* is in this matter an even more perfect example
of the influence of the drama working in the interest of
form. Every scene in the book takes place within the
horizon of one standing upon Rainbarrow, within the
compass of the heath, which is like a great stage gloomily
hung for tragedy. In *A Pair of Blue Eyes*, in *A Laodi-*

---

[1] There is also to be taken into account the influence of the short
story.

cean, in *Tess*, the range of the action is much wider, comprising all that falls within the more extended experience of the heroines, who have occasion to make journeys, to strike roots in soils diverse, and to undergo a considerable variety of conditions underneath the sky.

Only in *The Woodlanders* is there anything like the unity of tone and atmosphere that prevails in *The Native;* and in *The Woodlanders* there is nothing like the intensity and poetic concentration of effect. Every scene of *The Native* is overshadowed with the gloom, the loneliness, the savage permanence of the heath, which has so obstinate a way of assimilating men to its likeness instead of yielding to their will and working. It is clear that Mr. Hardy had very distinctly imagined, and went about very deliberately to evoke, the atmosphere with which he wished to envelop his tragedy. He has not written three pages before he bids us reflect whether this gloomy heath is not more in keeping with modern taste in landscape than "smiling champaigns of flowers and fruits."

Haggard Egdon appealed to a subtler and scarcer instinct, to a more recently learnt emotion, than that which responds to the sort of beauty called charming and fair. . . . . The new vale of Tempe may be a gaunt waste in Thule: human souls may find themselves in closer and closer harmony with external things wearing a sombreness distasteful to our race when it was young. The time seems near, if it has not actually arrived, when the chastened sublimity of a moor, a sea, or a mountain will be all of nature that is absolutely in keeping with the moods of the more thinking of mankind.

And if this author prefers an uncultivated waste for his typical reflection of modern thought, it is mainly in night and storm that he chooses to present it. The story opens, sadly adagio, at cloudy twilight in November, with the darkness of the heath drawing down night upon it before its time; and practically all the scenes that follow in the first book are in the blackness of night out of doors in the desert, starless, moonless, and with only the flicker of seasonal bonfires to add luridness and mystery to the figures of those who dance about the fire on Rainbarrow or talk in tense and muffled tones inside the bank and ditch of Captain Vye's at Mistover Knap. The brightest coloring which Hardy admits into this composition of blacks and browns is the green of fern fronds on a June day, proper to love-making. The story closes on another night in November, with "rain, darkness, and anxious wanderers" feeling their way across the featureless waste by the help of footsoles long used to paths that cannot be seen by the eye, and drawn together about the rain-flooded pool where men and women struggle for life in the dark.

No reader of Hardy need be reminded of the massive power and beauty of these scenes in which the darker pigments so predominate; nor of the shining splendor with which the points of brightness from candle or bonfire make their intense and brief assertion of light in a world of gloom. Only the etching needle of Rembrandt could do justice to the scene where Wildeve and Christian throw dice for gold pieces by the feeble light of a lantern amid the vast encompassment of the night-shrouded heath. First Christian and Wildeve playing by the light of the lantern; and then, when Christian has lost all, and the candle has been put out by the blind fluttering of a moth, Wildeve and Venn throwing dice upon a flat stone by the feebler light of glowworms ranged in a circle. And as ever with this poet of landscapes that are the stage of human action, there is the quiet insistence of poetic symbolism, in which the physical circumstances have their suggested counterpart in the disposition of men's hearts. "Both men became so absorbed in the game that they took no heed of anything but the pygmy object immediately beneath their eyes; the flat stone, the open lantern, the dice, and the few illuminated fern-leaves which lay under the light, were the whole world to them."

What we are concerned with here is the unity of tone—the steadiness with which the heath makes us feel its dark and overshadowing presence, so that men and women are but slight figures in a giant landscape, the insect-fauna of its somber flora. Mr. Hardy was bold enough to begin this grave history with an entire chapter devoted to a description of the heath at twilight; and his choice of a title for the second chapter but serves to signalize the littleness and frailty of man upon the great stage of inhospitable nature: "Humanity appears upon the scene, hand in hand with trouble." It is very quietly and without word or gesture that humanity makes its appearance, like a slow-moving shadow. "Along the road walked an old man. He was white-headed as a mountain, bowed in the shoulders, and faded in general aspect. . . . . Before him stretched the long, laborious road, dry, empty, and white."

The effect is obtained at this point by means too subtle for analysis. It may be that the gravely cadenced rhythm itself plays a mysterious part in rightly affecting the imagination. More often the effect can be traced largely to figures of speech of definite connotation.

The sights and sounds of man's activity the author is forever comparing to those of extra-human nature, assimilating them to the concert of natural sights and sounds.   In one place he has been describing the strange whispering emitted by the myriad, mummied heath bells of the past summer played upon by plaintive November winds.   It was like the voice of a single person, of a spirit, speaking through each in turn.   And then

. . . . Suddenly, on the barrow, there mingled with all this wild rhetoric of night a sound which modulated so naturally with the rest that its beginning and ending were hardly to be distinguished.   The bluffs, and the bushes, and the heather-bells had broken silence; at last, so did the woman; and her articulation was but as another phrase of the same discourse as theirs.

The movements of human beings are sometimes described as seen upon the horizon by someone watching, and in terms that suggest the motions and forms of the lower organic, or even of the inorganic, world.   Diggory Venn, for example, has been eavesdropping at a meeting of Eustacia and Wildeve, and at a certain point he loses sight of them.   "Their black figures sank and disappeared from against the sky.   They were as two horns which the sluggish heath had put forth from its crown like a mollusc, and had now again drawn in."   By various means the people of the story are made to seem, like the heath-croppers or wild ponies dimly discerned in the dusk, but as creatures of the heath.

8

It is Eustacia and Clym who by their strength of mind and will rise most above the lower orders of nature and most vigorously resist the leveling and absorbing forces of the heath. But that is the very source of the tragedy. Where souls content to submit to the stress of circumstance are like briars humbly bowing to the winds of fate, these great ones, obstinate in their strength of will, are broken like the oak tree of the fable. And it is more carefully for them than for any minor figures that the stage is set and hung by the dramatist. It is, we feel, for Eustacia that, in the first book, the author proceeds with such deliberation to make his massive evocation of night upon the heath. She is the "figure against the sky" that attracts the anxious speculative gaze of the reddleman. She is the "Queen of Night" —the witch, as the superstitious thought her—who dominates the lives of Thomasin and Wildeve. It is her lonely life, for one thing, that has given her that dignity and freedom from vulgarity that add beauty to the force of her emotions. And however much she may long for a gaiety and a largeness of opportunity not afforded by the life of seclusion, there is an artistic congruity between her environment and her dark and unconventional passions, her savage independence of mind. It will be the eternal irony of this poetic figure that no reader will ever be able to dissociate her from the lonely and gloomy setting from which she made her desperate vain attempt to escape.

As for Clym, it is another aspect of the heath with which he will be forever associated in the reader's imagination. He will be seen, in his leather garb, cutting furze in the hot afternoons of midsummer in the insect-haunted hollows of the heath. He will be seen as he was seen by his mother, a figure "of a russet hue, not more distinguishable from the scene around

him than the green caterpillar from the leaf it feeds on."
He had been pointed out to her, on her journey across
the heath, as one who could show her the way to the place
where she was going.

> The silent being . . . . seemed to be of no more account in
> life than an insect. He appeared as a mere parasite of the heath,
> fretting its surface in his daily labour as a moth frets a gar-
> ment, entirely engrossed with its products, having no knowledge
> of anything in the world but fern, furze, heath, lichens, and
> moss. . . . .

And then

> . . . . Suddenly she was attracted to his individuality by
> observing peculiarities in his walk. It was a gait she had seen
> somewhere before; and the gait revealed the man to her, as the
> gait of Ahimaaz in the distant plain made him known to the
> watchman of the king. "His walk is exactly as my husband's
> used to be," she said; and then the thought burst upon her that
> the furze-cutter was her son.

This obscure way of life was not unpleasant to the
man so lacking in wordly ambition. It was not inappro-
priate to the philosophy which he had come back to the
wilderness to preach. The very monotony of his labor
"soothed him. and was in itself a pleasure." And so
it happened that his wife could find him, on a summer
afternoon, singing at his work, a social failure and not
ill-content.

If his mother was shocked at the humble occupation
of the son for whom she had hoped great things, how
much sorer was the disappointment and distress of the
wife, who in this humiliation could read the death
sentence of all her aspirations for herself! The garb
and occupation were bad enough in themselves, symbol-
izing the return to the narrow way of life she hated.

But it was the cheerful mood of Clym that was hardest to bear, proving his willing surrender to the captivity of the heath. It was inevitable that hard words should be spoken, that bitterness and pride should come between them, that she should turn again, however reluctantly, to the thought of Wildeve. When the death of Mrs. Yeobright had brought upon her the jealous suspicion of Clym, it was natural that, in her pride, she should have withheld the words that might have cleared up the misunderstanding. And from that point to her suicide she was carried as on a resistless current flowing from her disillusionment.

It is thus that Egdon takes its place as the dominating force of the tragedy, as well as its appropriate and impressive setting. So that the unity of place, in itself an artistic value, is but the counterpart of a unity of action rooted and bedded in a precious oneness of theme. Instead of being, as in *Far from the Madding Crowd*, brought together arbitrarily to make out the prescribed materials of a novel, plot and setting here are one, growing equally and simultaneously out of the dramatic idea expressed in the title. For the first—and almost for the last—time in the work of Hardy, the discriminating reader is delighted with the complete absence of mechanical contrivance. Contrivance there is as never before in his work, the loving contrivance of an artist bent on making everything right in an orderly composition; the long-range contrivance of an architect concerned to have every part in place in an edifice that shall stand well based and well proportioned, with meaning in every line.

PART TWO: MORE CRAFT THAN ART

V. RELAPSE

The power and beauty of *The Return of the Native* stand out in most striking relief when it is viewed in connection with the long series of inferior works which followed, works on the whole so commonplace in conception and so flabby in execution that they drive us to some hypothesis of the demands of the market, exhausted imagination, or impaired physical vigor. Even when Mr. Hardy had recovered himself sufficiently to lay out the vigorous canvasses of *The Mayor of Casterbridge* and *The Woodlanders*, he was still far from recovering the technical power exhibited in *The Native*, or even, it may be judged by some, in earlier novels. Then follows the clear and serene mastery of *Tess*, to be followed again by the relative weakness of *The Well-Beloved* before the final triumph of *Jude*.

It might almost seem as if, after each display of knowledge and sureness of hand, the author had dropped back again into the groping experimental stage; and you are led to wonder at times whether he had ever consciously *learned* the technical refinements of his art, whether perhaps the formal perfection of *The Native* or of *Tess* might not be a mere happy accident. One would be practically constrained to this conclusion were it not for the progress in art manifested throughout the series of novels as a whole—*The Madding Crowd* so much finer than anything earlier, *The Native* so much finer than that, with *Tess* and *Jude* going so far beyond even *The Native* in perfection of art.

This is the most convenient place to take up in a group the six novels in which, at one time or another, he falls farthest below the standard set by himself, reserving for separate consideration *The Woodlanders* and *The Mayor of Casterbridge*, novels of a much higher quality, but examples of certain backward tendencies in novelistic art.

I

After the grave and beautiful work of *Far from the Madding Crowd*, Mr. Hardy diverted himself with an essay in comedy of rather dubious effectiveness, *The Hand of Ethelberta*. This story relates the campaign of Ethelberta Petherwin to dispose of her hand most advantageously. She is the daughter of a butler, but has been lifted into a higher social sphere by marriage with a gentleman, now deceased. The clever widow wishes to marry wealth in order to raise the fortunes of her numerous brothers and sisters. She turns her back on love in the person of a gentleman of good family but poor fortune, a musician. She goes to London and undertakes to scale society by means of her literary talent. She takes with her some of the family. A brother and a sister serve her in the capacities of butler and tire-woman; others are sturdy workmen, who help to decorate her house. With none of them can the would-be lady have any but secret communication. She has great social success, and is sought by various suitors—a distinguished painter, a rich clubman, a Lord of broad lands. She finally marries the Lord. He is an old Silenus; but she tames him, masters him, and has her will. Her nice younger sister Picotee is happily married to the musician-lover of Ethelberta. Picotee has been in love with him all along; but it is only after losing Ethelberta that he realizes the merits of Picotee.

It is likely that Mr. Hardy was aiming at something the tone of *Evan Harrington* or *Sandra Belloni*. But he has none of the comic afflatus of Meredith. He cannot command the burlesque vein in which the earlier novelist related the means by which the three "Daughters of the Shears" had raised themselves in the social sphere. There is no one to correspond to the Countess de Saldar or to the Pole sisters—no one so funny. Ethelberta is not funny at all, in spite of her comic rôle of social climber. She is merely the object of an irony that misses fire. It misses fire because, somehow, the author makes us take her seriously, though without arousing deep interest in her. Even when she goes secretly to inspect the estate of one of her suitors and is caught by him in the act, we are made to feel her chagrin rather than the ludicrous vulgarity of her performance. There is only the most perfunctory suggestion of her being subjected to an ordeal and being found wanting. We cannot feel for her the admiring sympathy we feel for Evan Harrington in his tardy triumph over snobbery, nor the amused scorn we feel for Wilfrid Pole when he succumbs to the seduction of a weak sentimentalism.

The humor is laid on in superficial patches. There is here and there a touch of satirical smartness that has a forced and hollow ring. It takes nearly a page to describe the boredom of people in a drawing-room compelled to listen to a song.

The sweetness of her singing was such that even the most unsympathetic honoured her by looking as if they would be willing to listen to every note the song contained if it were not quite so much trouble to do so. Some were so interested that, instead of continuing their conversation, they remained in silent consideration of how they would continue it when she had finished; while the particularly civil people arranged their countenances into every attentive form that the mind could devise.

And so he goes on ringing facetious changes upon this boresome theme. In dialogue the society people are somewhat heavily reminiscent of Congreve; the low comedy people echo weakly the fun of Charles Dickens or Dick Steele. Little fourteen-year-old Joey, the rustic butler of Ethelberta, explains the ways of the city to his sister Picotee, timid and fresh from the country. The main evidence of his social forwardness is his use of tobacco. When Picotee begs him not to smoke he answers gravely, "What can I do? Society hev its rules, and if a person wishes to keep himself up, he must do as the world do. We be all Fashion's slave—as much a slave as the meanest in the land!"

Much the most interesting part of the story is that toward the end where we are in doubt as to whether Ethelberta will be allowed to become the bride of the dreadful old rake. There is one long passage in which the musician-lover, her brother Dan, her father the butler, and a brother of Lord Mountclere are all making desperate efforts to get to Knollsea in time to prevent the marriage. It has an excitement like that of *Around the World in Eighty Days*. And then, after the wedding, having discovered something of the character of her husband, when Ethelberta plots with her faithful lover to escape by night and is baffled by the slyness of her

Lord, we have the excitement, danger, suspense, and physical action which have won popularity for many a story and many a play. When we say that this is the most interesting thing in the book, we have adequately measured the failure of this attempt at comedy.

2

The Trumpet-Major is another essay in comedy. But it cannot be called a failure, nor even strictly speaking an attempt. The author is no longer undertaking the satirical delineation of smart life, but is dealing with much more familiar and congenial matter— matter of Wessex indeed. And the historical subject gives scope to that devoted antiquarianism of the hermit of Dorchester which he has indulged in many of the short stories, as well as in the reconstructions of *The Greenwood Tree* and *The Madding Crowd*, and, in so scholarly a fashion, in *The Dynasts*.

The story is built around the excitement in a Dorsetshire coast village arising from the anticipated invasion by Napoleon in the early years of the nineteenth century, the same alarm that led the pacific Wordsworth to join a company of volunteers and gave occasion for several of his most ringing patriotic sonnets. It was the time when Majesty visited his favorite watering-place, when there was great drilling of the militia, and troops were encamped on the downs above the village. The heroine is a nice girl, Anne Garland by name, living with her widowed mother in the house of the local miller. The leading men are her three suitors, one a cowardly officer of the yeomanry, the other two brave men and brothers, John and Robert Loveday, the one a soldier and the other a sailor. John is the better man of the two, faithful, thoughtful, and generous. But it is the light-headed and incontinent Bob who has originally won the heart of the heroine, and who in the end, after various misunderstandings, is awarded the prize of her hand.

Readers of Hardy will not be surprised at such an outcome; and it is in the character of Anne and her dealings with the two brothers that he shows himself most like the Thomas Hardy of the great novels. This is all done, however, with a purposeful lightness of touch which bids us pass it over lightly. More care was apparently given to the historical details as they were to be gleaned from contemporary newspapers and chronicles and from the stories of old men in Mr. Hardy's youth. He takes great pains with the outfit and drilling of the yeomanry, the equipment of the soldiers, the equipage of the King; and it is evident that he introduces with great relish the incident of Nelson's death at Trafalgar—it was as officer upon the flagship "Victory," under Captain Hardy, that Bob Loveday won his spurs.

The plot is duly thickened with misunderstandings, and leads duly to moments of exciting action. More than once the heroine is in great danger from the attentions of her bullying lover of the yeomanry, and has to flee from him on foot or on horseback, and with her wits pitted against his in tricks and dodges. One time, by means of a displaced plank, she lands him splashing in the water like any victim of slapstick comedy. More exciting still are the circumstances of Bob Loveday's escape from the press-gang. This adventure involves much leaping out of window, sliding down ropes, and the like. But the most remarkable of Bob's feats is having himself raised from story to story of the mill by the chain for hoisting flour-sacks, and then letting go just soon enough not to be dashed against a beam at the top. His pursuers are ever close behind, and arrive at each story just in time to see his "legs and shoebuckles vanishing through the trap-door in the joists overhead." The reader of a certain age will remember having witnessed scenes like this in a type of melodrama now gone out of fashion, not to mention the dime novels of remote boyhood.

Two of the characters furnish a large amount of the comedy of "humors." Uncle Benjy, the miser, the sly fox, who is so in fear of his nephew Festus, and always treats him with such a show of affection and admiration; and the nephew Festus, the *miles gloriosus*, who is so bent upon winning the girl and on getting away with his uncle's money-box—these are traditional characters of English comedy in novel or play, with nothing to distinguish them from their kind from Ben Jonson down. Festus Derriman is an arrant coward, who is frightened almost to death when he hears that Napoleon has landed, but who, when he gets advance information that this is a false alarm, plays the part of a gallant leader for those who still believe the enemy is near. There is considerable broad comedy in the tricks played upon one another by him and his uncle; there are several long dialogues displaying his cowardice in mere anticipation of being called into action against the foe; and other amusing scenes in which his bluff is called. There are good lines for a Joe Jefferson, or one of the old comedians, as in a comedy of Sheridan or Goldsmith. And it is all sheer "literature," a passable exercise in a quite obsolete manner.

Much more of Hardy's world are the widow Garland and the miller Loveday. These amiable characters are drawn with mild and faithful humor; and it is a fine touch of country thrift when their nuptials are hastened to take advantage of the good things prepared for the wedding of Bob that failed to come off. In general the tone of the narrative is very pleasing, and especially in the playful and loving treatment of the old buildings and the old furniture, so impregnated with genial human history, and so genially eloquent of the "filings and effacements" of time. No one could have related with a mellower and more sympathetic humor the great housecleaning of the widow Garland; no one could have described with finer antiquarian gusto the ancient hall of Uncle Benjy. No one could have made us more in love with crack-walled, round-shouldered Overcombe Mill. And it is purely in gratitude that one marks as in the manner of Addison the droll history of Miller Loveday's family.

It was also ascertained that Mr. Loveday's great-grandparents had been eight in number, and his great-great-grandparents sixteen, every one of whom reached to years of discretion: at every stage backwards his sires and gammers thus doubled till they became a vast body of Gothic ladies and gentlemen of the rank known as ceorls or villeins, full of importance to the country at large, and ramifying throughout the unwritten history of England. His immediate father had greatly improved the value of their residence by building a new chimney, and setting up an additional pair of millstones.

The history as a whole is enveloped in a kind of mist of tender humor like the subtle mist of superfine flour which penetrated all chambers of the miller's house. And through it all there runs a pervasive tone of gentle elegy suggestive of Irving or of Goldsmith. That is also true Hardy; and the reader of *The Dynasts* will recognize a milder essence of the melancholy of that tragic panorama in the author's reflection on the disappearance of the troops encamped upon the downs.

They still spread the grassy surface to the sun as on that beautiful morning, not, historically speaking, so very long ago; but the King and his fifteen thousand armed men, the horses, the bands of music, the princesses, the cream-coloured teams—the gorgeous centre-piece, in short, to which the downs were the mere mount or margin—how entirely have they all passed and gone!— lying scattered about the world as military and other dust, some at Talavera, Albuera, Salamanca, Vittoria, Toulouse, and Waterloo; some in home churchyards; and a few small handfuls in royal vaults.

It is a light and pleasing confection, ingeniously compounded of many diverse materials—a graceful diversion and unbending of genius—not altogether unworthy of the hand that could do so much more serious work.

3

After *Desperate Remedies*, Mr. Hardy never again wrote a story of ingenuity pure and simple. This element does make its appearance, and rather far down the list of his novels, but always in combination. It appears in the rôle of dubious assistant to themes of some dignity and point, some real value for art. It is a crutch, a bit of machinery for making a go of stories which might be expected to interest the reader in quite a different way, but which seem unable to stand up, or to make progress, without such artificial helps.

Such a story is *A Laodicean*, which comes after *The Return of the Native*, but which, by this resort to machinery, makes confession of its weaker birth. The theme is one of no little promise. The Laodicean is a young woman of wealth and charm, one Paula Power, who finds herself in possession of a picturesque old castle enriched with family portraits of the Norman De Stancys. She is herself the daughter of a great railroad king who had been a civil engineer and donor of the local Baptist church, an edifice of characteristic ugliness; and she is thus the hereditary representative of everything most opposed to the mellow traditions of her domicile. She is in religion a Laodicean, unable to make up her mind either to be immersed in the proper Baptist fashion or to repudiate her father's faith. Socially and imaginatively she aspires to become everything that her castle stands for, and is thus strongly tempted to accept the hand of Captain De Stancy, the heir to the baronetcy. But her heart declares for plain George Somerset, the gifted architect who has been engaged to make the castle habitable. It is in this affair of her marriage that she chiefly earns her title of Laodicean—neither hot nor cold. It is long before the heart asserts its paramount claim.

It is a pretty theme, offering ample scope for the delineation of manners or the display of character—a theme for Thackeray, say, or Henry James. But it has not enough of "Wessex" for Mr. Hardy, and it has too much of smart life. Almost from the beginning he must have felt unequal to its challenge. It had already begun its race in the magazine; Mr. Hardy, as he tells us, was not well; the story must be continued, it must be strung out to its five hundred pages. The obvious thing to do was to introduce a villain (or several villains), a mystery (or several mysteries), and to set going complications and misunderstandings which should take time for clearing up and duly put off the hour of the happy ending.

Hence the introduction of young Dare, the mysterious wise boy, the illegitimate son of Captain De Stancy, who has the family name tattooed on his breast, and who threatens with his revolver the confederate who discovers that dread secret. It is Dare who steals Somerset's plans for the castle in order to secure his defeat in the contest with a local architect. It is he who manages to inflame his father with love for the heiress. It is he who falsifies photographs and sends "fake" telegrams in order to persuade Paula of the unworthiness of his father's rival. It is he who in the end sets fire to the family portraits and causes the burning down of the castle.

And not content with one villain, the author must needs provide another in the person of Paula's uncle Abner—not to mention the half-hearted villain, the architect Havill. Abner Power was no less than a notorious Red and maker of bombs, wanted by the police in most countries of Europe. It is a typical scene of melodrama when the two arch-villains cross swords (or literally pistols) across the vestry table of a church after attending a funeral. Power would like to get Dare out of the country, so as to save trouble for Paula and De Stancy. And he tries to persuade him by threats of exposing his criminal practices. Young Dare retorts by relating, in the form of a dream, the history of

Power, showing how completely, as we say nowadays, he has "got the goods on him." And having come to a deadlock in this form of argument, the adversaries resort to one more urgent and exciting.

Dare raised his eyes as he concluded his narration. As has been remarked, he was sitting at one end of the vestry-table, Power at the other, the green cloth stretching between them. On the edge of the table adjoining Mr. Power a shining nozzle of metal was quietly resting, like a dog's nose. It was directed point-blank at the young man.

Dare started. "Ah—a revolver?" he said.

Mr. Power nodded placidly, his hand still grasping the pistol behind the edge of the table. "As a traveller I always carry one of 'em," he returned; "and for the last five minutes I have been considering whether your numerous brains are worth blowing out or no. The vault yonder has suggested itself as convenient and snug for one of the same family; but the mental problem that stays my hand is, how am I to despatch and bury you there without the workmen seeing?"

"'Tis a strange problem, certainly," replied Dare, "and one on which I fear I could not give disinterested advice. Moreover, while you, as a traveller, always carry a weapeon of defence, as a traveller so do I. And for the last three-quarters of an hour I have been thinking concerning you, an intensified form of what you have been thinking of me, but without any concern as to your interment. See here for a proof of it." And a second steel nose rested on the edge of the table opposite to the first, steadied by Dare's right hand.

They remained for some time motionless, the tick of the tower clock distinctly audible.

Mr. Power spoke first.

"Well, 'twould be a pity to make a mess here under such dubious circumstances. Mr. Dare, I perceive that a mean vagabond can be as sharp as a political regenerator. I cry quits, if you care to do the same?"

Dare assented, and the pistols were put away.[1]

[1] P. 428.

This is a good sample of the cool and masterful, the high ironic manner, à la Dumas, in which our villains deliver themselves. It is true that not often in *A Laodicean* do we have a scene of such intense excitement. But there is throughout a quite sufficient provision of mystery and melodrama. There is a first-class concatenation of incidents, with well-sustained suspense. The average magazine reader must have been well satisfied; and few so much as realized the submergence, the total eclipse, of the excellent *subject*.

4

Quite similar is the case of *Two on a Tower*, the novel that followed *A Laodicean*. Here, too, Mr. Hardy has a very promising theme, and one much more congenial to his talent. He undertakes to record "the emotional history" of Swithin St. Cleeve, a very young man with a passion for astronomy, and Lady Constantine, older than he and with affections *disponibles*—her unsympathetic husband having been long absent in African exploration. On the top of a lonely fir-girt hill upon her Wessex property rises a memorial tower, suitable for the observation of the heavens; and Swithin St. Cleeve receives permission of Lady Constantine to use it for that purpose. There he sets up an "equatorial" glass provided by her munificence; there she visits her protégé and is initiated into the mysteries—the ghastly immensities—of the stellar universe. There is much of poetry and much of irony in their nocturnal converse. Lady Constantine is indeed more taken up with her own personal affairs than with those "impersonal monsters," the "voids and waste places of the sky"; and yet she cannot help being impressed and made to feel insignificant by Swithin's graphic exposition of the size of the universe.

It is Swithin's ambition to become the Copernicus to the systems beyond the solar system. And while she is falling in love with the Adonis, he is preparing to publish his great discovery in regard to the fixed stars. When he learns that he has been anticipated (by a paltry six weeks) by an American scientist, he falls into despair, lies in the damp, takes fever, is on the point of death, and is passionately kissed by Lady Constantine. He recovers, not, however, because of the lady's kiss, but because he has heard of a new comet, and that gives him a new interest in life. In the meantime Lady Constantine learns of the death of her husband, and is free to indulge her love for Swithin. There follows a sufficiently amusing scene between the lovelorn but modest lady and the naïve astronomer, conscious of nothing but the state of the heavens.

So there we have the subject of the book. "This slightly-built romance," says Mr. Hardy, "was the outcome of a wish to set the emotional history of two infinitesimal lives against the stupendous background of the stellar universe, and to impart to readers the sentiment that of these contrasting magnitudes the smaller might be the greater to them as men." He has succeeded in setting this history against that background, and perhaps to some degree has imparted to readers the desired sentiment. He has, moreover, set the stage for an amusing little comedy of the Scientist and the Loving Woman unequally yoked together by what Clough calls "juxtaposition." And then he largely abandons the comedy and the stellar background, and even the emotional history, in order to relate the surprising series of events by which the passion of Lady Constantine is baffled.

A secret marriage leads to various subterfuges and embarrassments when Lady Constantine is visited by her brother and the Bishop of Melchester. It is still worse when she learns that the death of her first husband had occurred actually six weeks after her marriage to Swithin, which will accordingly have to be repeated in order to be legal. And then she learns of a bequest made to Swithin for his scientific studies on condition that he remain single to the age of twenty-five. She determines to give him up, and he goes off to the southern hemisphere on a scientific mission of several years duration. After he has gone, poor Lady Constantine once more finds herself in trouble. It turns out that she is with child by Swithin, now no longer her husband. She makes a frantic effort to get into communication with him. And failing that, she is reduced to marrying the Bishop in order to legitimize her child.

The record of these events occupies nearly two hundred pages, or more than half the book. The last two chapters bring the history to its conclusion. After several years in Africa, learning of the death of the Bishop, the astronomer returns—being now of the prescribed age of twenty-five—to offer his hand to the lady. He finds her upon the tower, together with their golden-haired child. She has grown old and worn; but he will not fail in his sentimental duty, and he insists that he has come back to marry her. Thereupon Lady Constantine is moved too deeply by the consummation of all her hopes; and happiness kills her. Swithin, we realize, will marry Tabitha Lark, a blooming young thing who had earlier been introduced for this very purpose.

The conclusion is characteristic of Hardy in its irony. The general conception is worthy of the master; and there is a considerable flavor of him in the early chapters. But he fails to give us any "emotional history." He has not more than space to make us understand the marvelous concatenation of events. The psychology is of the most conventional, the simplest, and the crudest. Human emotions are secondary, and are manipulated in the most cavalier fashion so as to make plausible the predetermined acts and combinations of circumstance. The rôle of Swithin is to be that of a passionate scientist and indifferent lover, yielding reluctantly to the advances of a loving lady. And yet, in order to bring about the marriage called for by the plot—and, I suppose, to preserve the modesty of the lady—he is made to change rôles with her, and to propose their union himself. This is weakly motivated by Swithin's inability to carry on his work while uncertain of the success of his love. If we had first been convinced of the existence of his love, we should be more impressed with this example of the prime importance for the scientist of being able to do his work. *Two on a Tower* is the last striking instance in Hardy's novels of the undue dependence upon intrigue, with the consequent obscuration of theme.

5

If the case is not similar in *The Romantic Adventures of a Milkmaid*, it is simply because that little story cannot be said to have a theme of any sort. It is, if the truth must be told, the most arrant pot-boiler that was ever turned out by tired and harassed writer of novels.[1] It is not without its prettiness, especially in the early chapters, and should be prized for its location of the story in the fat valley of the Swenn, early study for Tess's Valley of the Great Dairies. But never was more simple and obvious the intention of carrying a plot through seventeen chapters with the greatest possible amount of change and surprise.

Margery Tucker, daughter of the dairyman, starts across the fields in the early morning, with a basket of fresh butter for her granny. Accidentally encountering in a summer house the mysterious foreign baron who has taken the great Place for the season, she saves him from suicide. This favor he repays by gratifying her wish to go to a yeomanry ball. She dresses for the ball in a hollow tree in the middle of the wood, and they roll off to the house of a nobleman in a neighboring county to dance the polka, then the rage, under the names of Mr. and Mrs. Brown. It is only on their return to the hollow tree that the baron learns from Margery of her engagement to Jim Hayward, master lime-burner; and by that time the sentiments, or imaginations, of milk-maid and baron have been somewhat touched.

How the baron backs the suit of the lime-burner; how he upsets everything by unwittingly preventing Margery from being present at her own wedding; how he summons her to his supposed death-bed and marries her to Jim, but on condition that she need not live with

[1] We ought in fairness to bear in mind that Mr. Hardy makes no claims for this work, which is covered by the apologetic, or deprecatory, tone of his prefatory note to *A Changed Man and Other Tales.*

her husband till she is ready; how by trickery Jim finally persuades his bride to come to his home—chiefly with a scarlet uniform and a pretended flirtation—such are the main incidents which bring the story up to the culminating scene of melodrama. The mysterious baron, essentially good and generous at heart, is not without his liability to temptation. And when he finds himself in a coach "blazing with lions and unicorns," together with a sweet country maid who is being taken, not very enthusiastic, to the home of her husband, what should he do but drive her to the coast and propose to carry her off on his yacht?

Then on a sudden Margery seemed to see all; she became white as a fleece, and an agonized look came into her eyes. With clasped hands she bent to the Baron. "Oh, sir!" she gasped, "I once saved your life; save me now, for pity's sake."[1]

There is a sample of the style at this exciting point in the story. The concluding paragraphs of the story are also good enough to quote. The life of Jim and Margery was a happy one; but the baron, it was rumored, at last effectually took his own life.

When she heard of his possible death Margery sat in her nursing chair gravely, thinking for nearly ten minutes, to the total neglect of her infant in the cradle. Jim, on the other side of the fireplace, said "You are sorry enough for him, Margery. I am sure of that."

"Yes, yes," she murmured. "I am sorry."

"Suppose he were to suddenly appear and say in a voice of command, 'Margery, come with me!'"

[1] I quote from p. 88 of the edition of the book in the Seaside Library published by George Munro in New York. This text is based on that of the original story in the *London Graphic*. It has been somewhat modified by Mr. Hardy for republication in 1913, as one may see by consulting p. 404 of *A Changed Man and Other Tales*.

"I believe I should have no power to disobey," she returned with a mischievous look. "He was like a magician to me. I think he was one. He could move me as a loadstone moves a speck of steel. Yet no," she added, hearing the baby cry, "he would not move me now."

"Well," said Jim, with no great concern (for "*la jalousie rétrospective*," as George Sand terms it, had nearly died out of him), "however he might move ye, my love, he'll never come. He swore it to me; and he was a man of his word."[1]

Little Red Riding Hood, Cinderella—the baron playing the double rôle of wolf and fairy godmother—and, for the rest, whatever was most to the liking of "The Duchess" and those other lady novelists who maintained throughout the nineteenth century the sentimental and Gothic traditions of the eighteenth!

6

While in *A Laodicean* and *Two on a Tower* the theme was overwhelmed by the forced complications of plot, the still more amazing pattern of circumstance which makes the plot of *The Well-Beloved* is, down to the least detail, the means of sharply defining, and we might say demonstrating, the theme. It is an interesting and characteristic theme, worked out with mathematical precision; and the book is worthy of a place on a shelf with the other novels of Hardy. But coming between *Tess* and *Jude*, it is wanting in strength and color. The first version, published in a magazine in 1892, is distinctly cruder than the revision of 1897, and strongly suggests the slapdash performance of a busy journeyman who has his bread to make from day to day, and is

[1] P. 90 in the Seaside Library volume; p. 406 in *A Changed Man and Other Tales*, somewhat revised.

saving his strength for some more cherished labor. In style and structure the book of 1897 shows a decided effort to raise the whole into a higher class.[1] But the care in revision cannot alter the fundamental fact that the thing is rather a poetic fantasy than a novel, a somewhat insubstantial, decidedly unconvincing invention, with a strong flavor of the *literary*. The theme is the stuff of poesy; and the plot which is invented to give it embodiment involves such surprising recurrence of similar situations as to tax the credulity of the most confirmed readers of Hardy.

It is a study in the artistic temperament as it is supposed to exhibit itself in love. The leading character, Jocelyn Pierston, is a sculptor, and the descendant of quarriers long settled in the peninsula known as the Isle of Slingers. And his descent from the "curious and almost distinctive people" of that isolated bit of Wessex, cherishing as they do "strange beliefs and singular customs," is another explanation of the fantastic dealings he has with the goddess Aphrodite, whose temple, according to tradition, "once stood at the top of the Roman road leading up into the isle." This young sculptor is one of those Shelleyan, platonic seekers of the ideal beauty, for whom it slips from form to form in the most freakish and uncontrollable fashion. Already at the age of twenty he has found the Well-Beloved embodied for him in no less than a dozen different women.

However it may have been with the ladies involved, the experience was not an unpleasant one to the artist himself; but it was destined to lead to complications,

---

[1] The differences are set forth in detail by Miss Chase in her Master's thesis before referred to.

and in the end to bring an ironic nemesis upon the involuntarily fickle man. The man of twenty, on returning to his native isle, finds himself in the, for him, unwonted situation of proposing marriage and becoming engaged to a nice girl of the ancient stock. It is doubtful whether the flitting ideal did ever take up its abode in the person of Avice Caro; but he is drawn to her by ties of intimate spiritual kinship, the growth of their common heredity. It is not long, however, before the true Well-Beloved casts her troublesome shadow over the sensible plans and engagements of Jocelyn Pierston. He falls in love with another daughter of the Isle, named Marcia, helps her in difficulty, takes her to London, and is going to be married to her. But before the marriage license can be obtained, the woman has changed her mind; and she passes out of the story for the space of forty years. Avice Caro marries a cousin of the same family name.

Such are the contents of Part First, entitled "A Young Man of Twenty."

Part Second is entitled "A Young Man of Forty," and shows us the first instalment of "Time's Revenges" upon the fickle artist-lover. The Well-Beloved has in the meantime had many incarnations; and she finally takes up her abode in a well-connected and accomplished society woman, who would make an ideal mate for the now distinguished sculptor. But he is not destined to such a tame and wordly-wise conclusion of his amorous career. Learning of the death of Avice Caro, he goes back to the Isle for her funeral. He meets there her daughter Avice, the very image of her mother. And this time there is no doubt that the phantom Aphrodite has descended upon the daughter of the woman whom he had wronged so many years before. They seem to his imagination one and the same person. His reason argues that it is not so, and that Avice the Second has not the soul nor the refinement of her mother. His reason points him away to the woman of fashion; but his tyrannical imagination insists on his paying court to the little laundress. It is a "gigantic satire upon the mutations of his nymph during the past twenty years."

And then, by a further stroke of irony, it appears that this bit of a rustic girl is now, as he had been, haunted by a phantom Well-Beloved, as flitting as his own, and as much beyond the control of her will. She has already loved no less than fifteen different men. The ironic moral was hardly in need of statement. "This seeking of the Well-Beloved was, then, of the nature of a knife which could cut two ways. To be the seeker was one thing; to be one of the corpses from which the ideal inhabitant had departed was another; and this was what he had become now, in the mockery of new Days."

But to complete the reversal of the situation, and squeeze out the last drop of irony, one further circumstance is called for. Avice being much troubled by the complications arising from her unstable imagination, Pierston takes her to London, hoping to save her from her troubles by making her his wife. But when at last he makes this purpose clear to the girl, she has to inform him that she is already married. Her husband is one of the island stock bearing his own surname, from whom she is at present separated because of her love for another man. Jocelyn Pierston has fully paid the penalty—whether to the first Avice for his instability, or to "the love-queen of the isle" for his reversion "from the ephemeral to the stable mood." The best he can do is to restore Avice to her husband and set them up in business on the Isle.

Such a plot would surely be remarkable enough in itself, and a sufficient illustration of the theme. But not content with this pretty reversal of parts, Mr. Hardy must needs give us a Part Third, with the hero appearing again as "A Young Man Turned Sixty," and a most miraculous reduplication of the events of Part Second. After another long interval, Pierston returns again to the Isle, and this time falls in love with Avice the Third, granddaughter of the first Avice Caro. She agrees to marry him to please her dying mother; but the night before the wedding she elopes with a former lover. This lover, by a final stroke of the playful malice of fate, is the son of Marcia, the beloved of forty years past. She has since been married and widowed, and has seen far countries. And then—to finish off the pattern with the last formal completeness—the artist and follower of flitting love marries the aged woman, loses altogether his sense of beauty, his artistic imagination, and settles down in his native isle as a useful and ordinary citizen.

It is all good fun. It is an idea quaintly conceived, and carried through without too much gravity. There is in the treatment of Pierston's obsession a note of levity, of light irony, rather well sustained. The obsession itself is not treated with any of the religious spirit of "Epipsychidion" or of the Italian poets of the *dolce stil nuovo;* and we are not expected to take in tragic mood the punishment meted out to the fickle lover.

There is a strain of poetry running through, but this is not of a sentimental order. It is found in the fanciful playing with the myth of an amorous divinity long established in the Isle. There are frequent references to the ancient goddess, "Aphrodite, Ashtaroth, Freyja, or whoever the love-queen of his isle might have been." The motif of the penalty recurs in various and not altogether reconcilable forms. And the artist's subjection to the Well-Beloved is itself represented as a kind of punishment. "Sometimes at night he dreamed that she was the 'wile-weaving Daughter of high Zeus' in person, bent on tormenting him for his sins against her beauty in his art." This mythical interpretation is indeed pushed too far. Mr. Hardy is not a Hawthorne; and he proves a little awkward in his attempt to suggest a supernatural mystery lurking in the background of his modern story.

There is considerable charm in the setting and atmosphere, the quaint stone houses, the quarries, the moan of the sea, the warmth of the rock in the sun— "that was the island's personal temperature when in its afternoon sleep." In social custom and material feature this is a special variety of Hardy's Wessex. But the local feeling is not so strong as in the greater novels. There is nothing like the dairying of Tess, the furze-cutting of Clym, the sheep-tending of Gabriel Oak, to give substantiality to the country and a deep local tincture to the characters. The characters are all phantoms, mere figures in the algebra of the theme.

It can hardly be otherwise with a plot so elaborately disposed of in so little space (for the book is a short one); a plot so marvelous and rigid in pattern, with so sharp an insistence upon so fantastic a theme. It has not the color and fulness of life. It pretends indeed to be no more than "a sketch of a temperament." It is good fun—one of the playful recreations of genius.

VI.   MOVIE

The Mayor of Casterbridge and *The Woodlanders* are
both works clearly impressed with the seal of genius,
the one a work of exceptional power, and the other a
work of exceptional charm.   But they are both books
in which it is hard to distinguish more than the most
rudimentary acquaintance with that art in the narrative
of events which was at the disposal of any well-read
novelist in the years 1886 and 1887.   There is only
one alternative to this conclusion: that the author may
in both cases have deliberately chosen, as proper to his
subject or congenial to his readers, a technique of slapdash facility and looseness.   In each case the subject
is one giving scope to a dramatic treatment similar to
that of *The Native;* but in each case the actual treatment
reminds one of the Elizabethan chronicle-play before
Marlowe and Shakespeare transformed it into tragedy.
The Mayor of Casterbridge departs even farther than
The Woodlanders from the method of sober and shapely
drama, reminding one often of the moving picture,
which has flourished so remarkably during the generation
following its appearance.

I

The Mayor of Casterbridge is a story dealing in
incidents of more than usual strangeness and improba-
bility, both in themselves and in their combination.
It covers a long course of years, and introduces so many
important events, so many amazing turns and complications, that four hundred pages are scarce enough

to get them told in a manner fully intelligible to the reader. A brief abstract can hardly fail to prove bewildering to anyone unacquainted with the book.

The story opens with no less an event than the sale of a wife. It is at a country fair that Michael Henchard, hay-trusser of imagination and of moody disposition, having come to realize how greatly he is burdened with wife and child, and being somewhat disguised in drink, turns jest into earnest, puts up his wife to auction, and knocks her down at five guineas to a seafaring man of chivalrous instincts. When, in soberer condition, he undertakes to recover his lost wife, his searching proves vain. He takes an oath not to touch liquor again within the space of twenty years; and he starts life afresh and unencumbered at the age of twenty.

Such are the contents of the first two chapters.

The story now takes a leap of eighteen years, and shows us Michael Henchard in great prosperity. He has become a prominent grain merchant of Casterbridge and mayor of the city. And by a strange coincidence, on the very night of the mayor's dinner, three strangers arrive in Casterbridge to witness his triumph. One is a young Scotchman named Farfrae, who is on his way to America to seek his fortune. He proves of service to Henchard in a business difficulty, and greatly takes the mayor's fancy by his pleasing personality; and he is persuaded by Henchard to stay in Casterbridge and become his partner.

The other new arrivals are no less than Henchard's wife Susan and her grownup daughter Elizabeth-Jane. It seems that the sailor has disappeared, and is thought to be drowned; and Susan has come back to seek out her lawful husband and secure, if possible, a father for her girl. Mayor Henchard, in spite of an awkward love-affair of his in the Island of Jersey, recognizes his obligation to his wife, and takes measures to give her her dues. He sets up the widow Newson in respectability in the town; and they play out together a prearranged comedy of getting acquainted and then getting married.

It is natural for young Farfrae to fall in love with his partner's daughter. But Michael Henchard is not a man whose acts are controlled by reason or good policy. He has grown jealous of the popularity of his partner; he finally dismisses him; and he forbids Elizabeth-Jane to have anything to do with a man who has now become a business rival and, in Henchard's view, "an enemy of his house." This is the situation at the time that Mrs. Henchard, for the convenience of the story, sickens and dies.

And now comes to the fore a complication which is destined greatly to affect the course of the history. Elizabeth-Jane is not really the daughter of Henchard. His daughter had long since died, and Elizabeth was the daughter of Newson. But Susan, to propitiate the jealous Henchard, has all along allowed him to believe that Elizabeth is his own flesh and blood. Meantime Elizabeth has been kept by them both in ignorance of the real facts about the original marriage and separation of Henchard and Susan, and of course supposes herself to be (as she is) the daughter of Newson. Wheels within wheels! But after the death of his wife, the lonely man, hoping to win the love of the girl, reveals to her, what he supposes to be the fact, that he is her father. And then, by one of those ironies of circumstance which he is ever provoking by his own perverseness, he comes immediately after upon a note from his dead wife confessing that Elizabeth is the daughter of Newson. It is his turn for concealing the facts of her birth; and he does not let the girl know of his mistake. The result is another irony. Elizabeth, who was at first greatly hurt by the thought that Newson was not her father, becomes reconciled to that fact, and turns her affections to Henchard, only to find that he apparently hates her. He really does hate her now for not being his daughter; and in this mood he gives Farfrae full permission to court her.

And next, having done his duty by his wife, Henchard is confronted by his obligations to his mistress. Everything repeats itself in the pattern of this plot. And no sooner is one past disposed of than another turns up to plague him. Lucetta, his Jersey love, having come into some money, has moved to Casterbridge and set up an establishment; her reputation has been damaged and she hopes to have it mended by Henchard. And thence grows another irony. For no sooner has Henchard determined to marry Lucetta, who is still attractive and now a person of means, than she has ceased to desire him, having fallen in love with Farfrae, his rival in business. And Farfrae, having received permission to love Elizabeth-Jane, loves instead Lucetta, who— though he knows it not—is so deeply engaged with the other man. The jealousy of Henchard is aroused; and he who had opposed the loves of Farfrae and Elizabeth, now opposes those of Farfrae and Lucetta. He uses his knowledge of Lucetta's past to compel her to promise marriage to himself.

Then at last comes his nemesis upon the man who has sold his wife and made an enemy of his friend. He has reached the summit of good fame; he has been mayor, and is still magistrate. But while he is sitting in dignity to pronounce judgment upon malefactors, a wretched old woman is brought before the court for some low offense. And who should she be, of all persons in the world, but a witness of Henchard's crime of many years before, the very woman who had sold him the drink that had made him reckless in wrongdoing? And what should she do, in her envious hatred of worldly respectabilities, but denounce the judge for his own crimes? Henchard impetuously acknowledges in open court the truth of her charges, and that he is no better than the prisoner at the bar. He is disgraced in the eyes of all men.

And now disgraces and disappointments crowd upon him. On the next day he learns of the secret marriage of Lucetta to his enemy. Farfrae has beaten him likewise in the business game, and he becomes a bankrupt. It is now twenty years since the sale of his wife; the date of his oath has expired, and he takes to drink. He is degraded to a common laborer, and must work for his former rival, whom he had once set up in business, and who now occupies Henchard's fine house and has been appointed mayor. He reaches the lowest depth of humiliation on the occasion of the King's visit to Casterbridge. He has determined to assert his dignity at this time by joining with the honorable Council in greeting Royalty. But in this purpose he is prevented by Mayor Farfrae, and hauled away by the collar in the presence of the whole town. And he hears himself described, by the woman to whom he had formerly condescended, as a mere workman employed by her husband.

It is at this period that Henchard is sorely tempted to get even with his enemies by violence and treachery. At one time he is on the point of killing Farfrae by throwing him out of an upstairs door in the barn; but he repents him before it is too late. At another time he is tempted to betray Lucetta by reading to her husband her old letters to himself. He does go so far as to read the letters to Farfrae; but his heart fails him at the last moment, and he does not reveal the identity of the writer. By mischance, however, he is the cause of disgrace to Lucetta. He undertakes to send back to her the incriminating letters. But the messenger he has chosen is a man with a deep grudge against both him and Lucetta; he reads the letters aloud in a public house. The result is that the scum of the town perform for the mayor's wife the scandalous ceremony of the "skimmity-ride." Following an ancient custom, they parade through the streets the grotesque effigies of Lucetta and Henchard, thus publishing their shame. And the disgraced woman dies soon after as a result of her agitation.

We now enter upon the last stage of the career of Michael Henchard. Elizabeth-Jane has come to be the comfort of her supposed father. And with her help and by the generosity of Farfrae, Henchard sets up again in a small way as a seed merchant. But now falls upon him another bizarre stroke of destiny; and once again he provokes the worst results by his unscupulous attempt to seize happiness for himself. With the disposal of

Susan and Lucetta, he has still to reckon with the sailor man, the father of Elizabeth. Newson turns out to have been alive all the time, and finally makes his appearance in Casterbridge. Henchard gets rid of him for the moment by telling him that Elizabeth is dead. And for a brief time he settles down to be the gentle father of an affectionate daughter. But Newson comes back again with a knowledge of Henchard's lie.

And that is not all; for now the ever triumphant rival, in business and love, who had taken his Lucetta from him, is about to take his Elizabeth-Jane. Upon the reappearance of Newson, Henchard has left Casterbridge; he returns for the wedding of Elizabeth and Farfrae. But the girl's heart has been hardened by the discovery of his duplicity. Against her arraignment he makes no appeal. He leaves her quickly with a promise never to trouble her more.

And he dies soon after of a broken heart.

2

It is with such hardihood that the author grapples with the crude stuff of men's lives, appalled by no circumstances or concatenation of circumstances, however violent and surprising. The reader's breath is almost taken away by the succession of surprising turns of the kind so much prized in a certain kind of romance, and now become the staple of the movies. Everything is so disposed that the story shall never lag, that never shall there be a failure of good things for the lover of movement and novelty. That a man should offer his wife at auction and find a buyer in the first chapter;

that his long-lost wife should return at the moment of his worldly triumph; that she should be so conveniently disposed of at so early a stage in order to make way for the other woman and all the complications that follow in her train; and she in turn for the sailor man, so long held in reserve by ironic fate; that the old woman who witnessed the sale of the wife should turn up so opportunely at the moment when she is required to complete the degradation of Henchard: these are but the most obvious and striking arrangements for providing plot in the highest degree of excitement and complication. Some are unusual enough in truth or fiction, and some of ancient hackneyed use in story— the mysteries and dubieties of birth, and the return of embarrassing relatives long put out of mind or thought to be dead. The combination is at any rate intriguing and bizarre.

Innumerable are the minor coincidences that contribute to the embroilment: that Jopp, for example, the man discharged by Henchard and refused the favor of her grace by Lucetta, should by chance have lived in Jersey in the earlier days and known of their love affair, and that he, the haunter of low taverns, should be the man to whose hands were intrusted the incriminating letters. There are many of those coincidences in which several persons whose fates cross come together strangely in the same place at the same time. Such is the chance by which Susan and Elizabeth are at the Three Mariners Inn on the very evening that Henchard and Farfrae meet there for their momentous interview; the dramatic chance by which Henchard, Elizabeth, and Farfrae meet at Lucetta's home, Farfrae being unaware of the acquaintance of Lucetta and Henchard; the melodramatic chance by which Henchard finds Lucetta and Elizabeth in the field with the mad bull, so as to save their lives on the very day on which he is to learn of Lucetta's secret marriage. And then there are those chances which throw a light so ironic upon human nature and its ineffectual commerce with fate: such as the return of Newson to deprive Henchard of the affections of Elizabeth just at the moment when the two have come to love each other.

And in addition to the ordinary patterns of coincidence and irony, there are many special devices sacred to the makers of plots since the beginning of time. Such is the mechanical means by which Farfrae and Elizabeth were brought together by Susan, the duplicate anonymous notes in which each one is requested to repair at the same moment to the same place, a method of bringing lovers together reminiscent of Beatrice and Benedick in *Much Ado*. Twice the author resorts to the old dodge of having one character tell his own story to another without giving names, thus adding a further spice of intrigue to the already much complicated plot.

And as for the overheard conversation, Mr. Hardy seems to have leaned more heavily on this feeble prop in *Casterbridge* than in any novel since *Desperate Remedies*. Elizabeth-Jane and her mother overhear the business talk of Henchard and Farfrae at the tavern; Lucetta overhears Henchard's reading of her letters to Farfrae; and Henchard seems always to be so placed behind wall or haystack as to hear news that maddens him and drives him on to fateful action.

3

All that is an old story with Hardy, though it is an element less in evidence in his more artistic performances. But the specialty of *The Mayor of Casterbridge*, and what makes its close affinity to the movie, is the large provision of scenes of violent and surprising action making their appeal directly to the sense of sight.

One of the chief and characteristic merits of a moving picture is that it shall tell its story with the least possible help from printed legend. Most perfectly adaptable to such purposes are three exciting scenes in which Henchard is the main actor: that in which he saves the two women from the onset of the bull; that in which he is prevented from greeting the King; and that in which he struggles with Farfrae by the open door of the barn and just fails to throw him down to destruction. No legend at all is required to elucidate the meaning of this kind of picture. It is not a matter of dialogue and debate; it is a simple affair of physical action proper to the life of the "wild west." The skimmity-ride, again, and the scene in which Henchard and Elizabeth discover the telltale effigies in the river, are suitable to that kind of pageantry which sets forth its meaning in visible symbols. Only slightly more in need of explanatory legend are the scenes connected with the sale of the wife—the auction itself in the first chapter, and the denunciation of Henchard for the act in open court—both so well adapted to the tastes of the movie audience by the agreeable shock they give the nerves. There are many other "dramatic" scenes requiring some complement of dialogue, but hardly more than the author actually supplies: the scene at the mayor's dinner where Henchard is challenged by a voice of discontent in regard to the "grown wheat" and makes his witty defiant reply; that in which he compels Lucetta to promise marriage; and the touching scene of his farewell to Elizabeth-Jane.

Mr. Hardy, as we have long since learned, takes firm hold upon the visible and tangible world, and we are at every point well supplied with objects to catch the eye and physical action suited to hold the attention. The device of the overheard conversation is a favorite one in the movies, it gives such scope for that study of facial expression which is so important a feature of movie art. Consider, for example, the picture that Henchard makes as he listens to the love-making of Farfrae and Lucetta, or later to that of Farfrae and Elizabeth. Or consider the opportunity given an "emotional actress" by the part of Lucetta listening to the talk of the servants across the street as they describe the skimmity-pageant.

It has been for Lucetta a day of triumph, the day of the King's visit, and she is waiting in the firelight for the return of her husband. Then her attention is suddenly called to the talk of the maids; and gradually as they describe the figures representing herself and Henchard, she comes to realize the horrible significance of this ceremony. We can imagine how her face passes by degrees from an expression of pleased reminiscence and tender pensiveness to one of dread and consternation. And then the action: "Lucetta started to her feet; and almost at the instant the door of the room was quickly and softly opened. Elizabeth-Jane advanced into the firelight." Elizabeth, hoping to spare Lucetta,

makes an attempt to close the shutters; but she is
forcibly prevented by Lucetta, who is determined, in
her agony, to hear and see the worst. They struggle
together . . . .

Elizabeth-Jane was frantic now. "Oh, can't something be
done to stop it?" she cried. "Is there nobody to do it—not one?"

She relinquished Lucetta's hands, and ran to the door.
Lucetta herself, saying recklessly, "I will see it!" turned to the
window, threw up the sash, and went out upon the balcony.
Elizabeth immediately followed her, and put her arm around her
to pull her in. Lucetta's eyes were straight upon the spectacle
of the uncanny revel, now advancing rapidly. The numerous
lights around the two effigies threw them up into lurid distinct-
ness; it was impossible to mistake the pair for other than the
intended victims.

"Come in, come in," implored Elizabeth; "and let me shut
the window!"

"She's me—she's me—even to the parasol—my green
parasol!" cried Lucetta, with a wild laugh as she stepped in.
She stood motionless for one second—then fell heavily to the
floor.[1]

One imagines perfectly how this would be managed
in the moving picture—the alternate showing of the
scene in the street and the scene in the house: the
grotesque figures representing the exposed man and
woman, and the actual face of the woman; the struggle
with Elizabeth; the bursting out on the balcony; again
the effigies as she sees them and her white face of anguish;
the puppet with the green parasol and the crowd of
onlookers; the stepping back from the balcony and her
fall to the floor. Here is no stately and deliberate stage
with high antagonists pitted against each other in a war
of measured words that are winged thoughts. Here is

[1] Pp. 337–38.

the vivid art of startling pictures full of movement, constantly shifting, and never failing in excitement and variety.

4

It goes without saying that the drama proper is most inadequately put before us. The story is told in outline, just enough so that the reader may keep abreast of the action, may take in what is meant; never lingeringly, so that he may get the relish, the intimate significance, the sense of being on the inside.

The difference will be startlingly apparent to a reader familiar with Trollope or George Eliot, Dostoyevsky or Meredith or Stevenson. Anyone who remembers Mrs. Proudie's reception in *Barchester Towers*, with the dramatic arrival of the Signora Vicineroni, knows what is meant by the full development of a comic situation. Anyone who has read the account of Hetty's journey in *Adam Bede* knows how the heart may be wrung by following at length the mental experiences of a human being in misery and despair. Anyone who has read of the visit of the Brothers Karamazov to the holy man, or the rapid succession of dialogues on the lawn following the discovery of Sir Willoughby's secret by Crossjay Patterne, knows how one place and one moment may burgeon out into clusters of scenes each more intriguing than the last. It all comes back to what Henry James calls "economy" in the use of material.

Of such economy Mr. Hardy had shown more than a notion in *A Pair of Blue Eyes* and *The Native*, as he was destined to show it again in *Tess* and *Jude*. But in *The Mayor of Casterbridge* he wastes his substance in the most riotous fashion. To take one example: the feeling of Henchard and Elizabeth toward one another after the death of Henchard's wife and Elizabeth's mother is a subject teeming with possibilities for such imaginations as James's or George Eliot's. It is indeed a subject of the greatest delicacy, and one calling for the most patient and thoughtful elucidation in order to have any value for story, for psychology, or for art. Above all the emotional experience of Elizabeth on the night following Henchard's announcement that he is her father, and his sudden change of heart upon learning that he is not her father—these are occurrences that need more than the dry statement of fact, the mere assertion by the author in the briefest of terms. Henchard's revulsion of feeling, in particular, would have required, one would suppose, more than a night to bring it about; and it certainly required more than his wife's letter and the glimpse of Elizabeth's features by candle-light to make us appreciate it as a psychological fact. But Hardy is concerned with nothing further, on the side of art, than the *irony* involved in the double and contrary change of heart; and he leaves the reader almost as puzzled as Elizabeth-Jane.

It is true that we have here some half-dozen pictures admirably adapted to the screen.

And something of the sort may be said for the book as a whole. There is matter here for half a dozen novels; but what is given is hardly more than the scenario of a movie.

5

Well then! many a reader will exclaim, so this is no more than a crude counterpart in print of the crude and vulgar art of the cinematograph! And can this be one of the valued works of a writer of genius, whom we prize among our thinkers and poets? There can be little question that *The Mayor of Casterbridge* is among the half-dozen most powerful novels of Thomas Hardy, only a little below *The Madding Crowd* and somewhat above *A Pair of Blue Eyes* in the serious appeal of its art. And this is almost wholly due to the character of Michael Henchard—the profound interest we take in him, and the entire faith we have in his existence. The first thing we realize when we begin to reflect upon any serious work of Hardy's is the unqualified honesty of his treatment of human nature. However romantic he may be in his plots, however ready to admit the sensational and improbable in combinations of incident, he maintains throughout his realism, his fidelity, in reference to the characters. The surest thing about Michael Henchard is that he is true to life. What happens to him may be incredible; he never loses, through whatever maze of action and intrigue, the simple integrity of his nature.

Mr. Hardy has never learned, it seems, the polite art of flavoring character to suit the public taste. He has not the recipe for a hero, or the still simpler recipe for a villain. He has none of those easy tricks for enlisting our sympathy for characters who are later to crave indulgence. The first moral item furnished in regard to Henchard is the evidence in his gait of "a dogged and cynical indifference." We see him trudging along with his wife in complete silence, accepting phlegmatically her suggestion as to a place for refreshment at the fair, developing a bitter loquacity under the influence of drink, and sullenly putting through the business of

auctioning off his wife and child. And yet we are
satisfied that we have here no exceptional brute, let
alone a despicable villain. We are not asked to look
upon this man as a Daniel Quilp or a Bill Sikes. The
author does not get excited, does not by word or gesture
call upon us to take sides against him; but by a kind of
sober evenness and candor of tone suggests that here is
something sad and not unnatural, which has its explanation in familiar experience. We can even feel the weight
of what the young hay-trusser has to urge about his early
imprudent marriage, and how it has prevented him from
getting on in life. It is not Henchard but an impartial
philosopher in the company who puts forth the suggestion
that "men who have got wives, and don't want 'em,
should get rid of 'em as these gipsy fellows do their old
horses." And public opinion is not made to interpose
a protest from any of the rustic company who witness
the transaction.

And as Hardy does not raise an outcry over the
selling of the wife, so he does not expatiate on the good-
ness of heart of Henchard in his long search for the lost
woman. It was a matter of course that he should have
more than spent in trying to find her the five guineas he
had received from her buyer; that he should have
followed patiently until the trace grew faint at the edge
of the ocean. It was what any man would have done
who had any feeling, any sense of obligation. It was
what any decent man would have done. And Michael
Henchard was decidedly a decent sort of man. The
author does not tell us that in so many words, but he
creates an atmosphere of truth, of fairness, in which we
form an opinion not colored by romantic predilections.

It is not often that an English author is so frank about his hero. And the absolute frankness of the author has much the same effect upon a thoughtful reader as frankness on the part of the character himself. It prepossesses the reader in favor of the character. And, for that matter, Henchard is frank enough, and severe enough, in judging of his own behavior. This was realized by Elizabeth when, after her wedding, she discovered the bird cage with the dead goldfinch, his neglected tribute of affection. The caged bird, she realized, "had been brought by Henchard as a wedding gift and token of repentance. He had not expressed to her any regrets or excuses for what he had done in the past; but it was a part of his nature to extenuate nothing, and live on as one of his own worst accusers." Altogether characteristic, again, was his acknowledgment in open court of the charge of the furmity woman. It had been pointed out by the other magistrate that her revelation had no bearing on the case before them, and the clerk had declared it to be a concocted story. It might easily have been denied by Henchard. But instead, in excess of self-abasement, he made his impetuous confession, and even agreed with the obscene creature that it did prove him no better than she and having no right to sit in judgment upon her. And he was capable of much harder and less theatrical a method of self-punishment. His remarriage with Susan was dictated by conscientious and almost morbidly sacrificial motives.

But it is by his warmth of nature that he takes hold upon our feelings. He is of the race of Tom Jones and not of Blifil. He can be cruel and violent, but never with deliberation. He may plot revenge and meanness; but when it comes to the scratch, he is constrained to fairness and generosity. He treats himself to the grim pleasure of reading to Farfrae the letters of the false Lucetta, and hearing her condemnation from the mouth of her husband and his rival; he has anticipated the delight of reading out her name with grand effect as the catastrophe of this drama. "But sitting here in cold blood he could not do it. Such a wrecking of hearts appalled even him. His quality was such that he could have annihilated them both in the heat of action; but to accomplish the deed by oral poison was beyond the nerve of his enmity."

And so with his sparing of Farfrae's life in the barn. Only think how he must have suffered in his vanity from the successes of Farfrae, whose very kindnesses were dagger-stabs to the sensitive self-respect of the fallen man! And now he has him at his mercy, the enemy of his house, who has taken away his woman, whom he has to obey as his master, and who has shamed him in the sight of all the town! Farfrae bids him take his life. "Ye've wished to long enough!"

Henchard looked down upon him in silence, and their eyes met. "O Farfrae!—that's not true!" he said bitterly. "God is my witness that no man ever loved another as I did thee at one time. . . . . And now—though I came here to kill 'ee, I cannot hurt thee! Go and give me in charge—do what you will—I care nothing for what comes of me!"

There is the simple accent of Bible truth. It is true that Henchard had loved Farfrae with all the heat of a passionate nature. He had carried Farfrae off his feet in the beginning by the naïve charm of his sudden affection. He had taken possession of him—not so much because he needed him in business as because he craved him in his lonely heart. He had taken possession of him, as friend took possession of friend in the early ages of the world, in places beyond the reign of caution or convention; he had taken him to his bosom, and loaded him with favors, and set him in high place. . . . . Only at last to grow jealous and unreasonable, to thrust him away in his perversity, and force him into the position of a foe!

For Michael Henchard was not a man governed by good policy. It would have been the best policy to secure Farfrae for his son-in-law. "But such a scheme for buying over a rival had nothing to recommend it to the mayor's headstrong faculties. With all domestic *finesse* of that kind he was hopelessly at variance. Loving a man or hating him, his diplomacy was as wrong-headed as a buffalo's. . . . ." It is this indeed which makes him so picturesque a figure, so good a hero of romance after all. He has not the colorless monotony of the business man who follows sure ways to success, who has conformed to every rule of conventional wisdom, and made himself as featureless as a potato field, as tame as an extinct volcano. Michael Henchard is the volcano in action. His is the impetuous, undisciplined, self-revealing nature of a child. And he fascinates us like the childish, picturesque people of Gorky and Dostoyevsky.

Like the characters of the Russian novel, Henchard gives the impression of being unreasonable and inconsistent. We come to expect of him freakish action, and to take it as a matter of course. But a careful examination of his conduct will show it is not at bottom inconsistent. His acts are wrong-headed enough, showing an incorrect analysis of the situation, inaccurate reading, or wilful ignoring, of their natural effects. But they all have their root in what is perhaps the most constant and powerful of all human passions—the passion of vanity. It is with him the frank vanity of a child—the craving for dignity and consideration which, in maturity, finds so many indirect expressions and disguises. There is little nobility in it, and little baseness. We all, when we are honest, recognize it in ourselves as perhaps the governing motive of action. And Hardy makes us honest. So that we are bound to have for his protagonist an indulgence like that we accord ourselves.

And then he is so blundering and childish in his struggle for consideration! He is his own worst enemy, the well-meaning author of his own failure. His failure is so complete and pathetic, and his acknowledgment of it couched in terms so simple and absolute! When they came upon his body in the lonely hut on Egdon Heath, Elizabeth and Farfrae found with it a penciled will, to the following effect:

That Elizabeth-Jane Farfrae be not told of my death, or made to grieve on account of me.

& that I be not bury'd in consecrated ground.

& that no sexton be asked to toll the bell.

& that nobody is wished to see my dead body.

& that no murners walk behind me at my funeral.

& that no flours be planted on my grave.

& that no man remember me.

To this I put my name.

MICHAEL HENCHARD[1]

[1] P. 404.

How pitifully he makes renunciation of all the posthumous dignities and satisfactions of mortality! None can harden his heart against him now. However he may have repelled us by his perversities in earlier stages of his career, he has at last won by his sufferings and his humanity a sympathy as whole-hearted as that we accord to King Lear, another violent and unreasonable figure of Wessex story.

6

And if Michael Henchard is a convincing and appealing figure, he is one well cast for his part in a story that is so like a moving-picture film. He is, after all, beneath his civil garb and chain of office, the original caveman, ever readier with blows than words. He is, amid the conventions and refinements of polite intercourse, a bull in a china shop; and his gentlest movement is accompanied by the crash of breaking crockery. He is more given to feeling than to thought; he does not arrive at decisions by the deliberate and tortuous route of reflection, reaching his position by due and gradual stages of approach.

In a world of talk, he is almost inarticulate. And we cannot expect to find, in any exchange of sentiments in which he takes a part, that slow arrival at the point at issue, that feeling of the way, that jockeying for position, that long ghostly fencing-match of allusion, before the opposed parties come to a grapple, which gives its breathless interest to so many a dialogue of Paul Bourget or Henry James. There is seldom any swaying back and forth of the opposed interests, any sustainment of the struggle by the arrival of reinforcements to one side or the other. The battle is soon joined and quickly over, and the field cleared for a new engagement. Michael Henchard is not the man to indulge in preliminary flourishes or diplomatic *pourparlers*. If he is not ready to do business, he has nothing to say; he stays at home. When he goes forth, it is because he is ready to do business.

It might be imagined that when he saw Lucetta again after so long a time, however well he may have made up his mind to propose the marriage that she has come to Casterbridge to bring about, he might have made his approaches to the subject with some decency of ceremony; he might have allowed their long-interrupted friendship a chance to re-establish itself. Any other author would have shown us his characters reaching out to one another with groping gestures. In Henry James, in Mrs. Wharton or Mr. Moore, there would have been some pretense, on one side or other, of tenderness, of lingering affection, before the matter was brought to a strictly business basis. But this is not the way of Michael Henchard. On his first visit to Lucetta—on the first occasion when he can speak to her alone—he marches straight up to his lady, brushes aside her "nonsense" about his politeness in calling, and delivers his precise and compact statement of intention.

"I've called to say that I am ready, as soon as custom will permit, to give you my name, in return for your devotion, and what you lost by it, in thinking too little of yourself and too much of me; to say that you can fix the day or month, with my full consent, whenever in your opinion it would be seemly: you know more of these things than I."

So there you have it, all in a breath. There is not much left to be said. And we read on the very next page that, as the result of a still more direct question of Henchard's, "Lucetta had the move." As we know, she did not at that time want to make the move, since her interest in Farfrae had come to make her indifferent to Henchard. There are endless possibilities of dramatic fencing in that circumstance; but within another page our impatient author has got rid of his impatient hero, and has left his heroine to make a final picture for his storied screen.

> He had hardly gone down the staircase when she dropped upon the sofa, and jumped up again in a fit of desperation. "I will love him," she cried passionately [meaning Farfrae]; "as for *him*— he's hot-tempered and stern, and it would be madness to bind myself to him knowing that. I won't be a slave to the past— I'll love where I choose!"

On his next visit Henchard meets Farfrae at Lucetta's and cannot talk to her alone. And there is no further interview recorded until one night many months later. It is after Henchard has witnessed the love-making of Farfrae and Lucetta in the harvest field; and she finds the jealous man awaiting her in her house. She complains of the impropriety of this late visit; and there is mutual recrimination to the extent of a little more than a page, bringing them to the subject of her reluctance to marry Henchard. He makes at last a reference to Farfrae, "The man you are thinking of is no better than I." And suddenly we arrive at the stage of the cinema.

> "If you were as good as he is you would leave me!" she cried passionately.

This unluckily aroused Henchard. "You cannot in honor refuse me," he said. [And then, as if there were nothing more to be said on that subject, and without further introduction:] "And unless you give me your promise this very night to be my wife, before a witness, I'll reveal our intimacy—in common fairness to other men!"[1]

All in a nutshell—reduced to the dimensions of a movie legend. Nothing more is said. "Without another word she rang the bell, and directed that Elizabeth-Jane should be fetched from her room." In the presence of Elizabeth-Jane the distracted woman agrees to marry Henchard and straightway falls into a faint. There is some bewilderment and protest on the part of Elizabeth; but in less than a minute her father is gone, and Lucetta has begged her to "let it all be."

So that is what Mr. Hardy does with the one situation in his novel that offers an opportunity for "scenical" development. That is all the use he makes of the delicate and dramatic relationship between his leading man and his leading woman. It is a waste of material at which other novelists would stand aghast—a want of refinement in method which must have been the amazement of certain of his contemporaries.

And yet who shall say it is not in its way effective art? Who shall say that Michael Henchard is not made to live as few figures live in history or fiction? Have we not seen him in action, in a hundred characteristic poses? So vivid is the presentation by this method of pictured moments, so complete and moving the illusion of life, that we well nigh forget the rude contrivances and violent shifts by which a plot was patched together.

[1] P. 236.

VII. CHRONICLE

It is our somewhat invidious task in this part of our study to measure the comparative failure of a great artist in some of his work by the standard of achievement set by himself in his best. We are particularly engaged in this and the preceding chapter in tracing the lapse in *The Mayor of Casterbridge* and *The Woodlanders* from the dramatic ideal as embodied in *The Return of the Native*. In *The Mayor of Casterbridge* we dwelt upon certain features suggestive of the moving picture. *The Woodlanders*, though wanting a Michael Henchard, is very similar to its predecessor in narrative technique; and we shall be occupied in this chapter with the illustration, from the later book, of other points in which both books fall short of the dramatic ideal—points which suggest indeed a kind of play which had its vogue in England before the evolution of a better form.

I

The theme of *The Woodlanders* has many points of likeness to that of *The Return of the Native*. The story concerns a young woman born to the rude and simple life of the remote woodland country, and attached to this life by all that is deepest in her emotional nature, but, through education and the ambition of her well-to-do father, turned aside from woodland ways and woodland associations, and aiming at a life of higher worldly standards. Such is Grace Melbury, daughter of the timber merchant, just returning, as the story opens, from her fashionable school to her father's home in Little Hintock. And the opposed ideals of the worldly and the woodland life are embodied in her two suitors, Edgar Fitzpiers, the local physician, philosopher, gentleman, and libertine, and Giles Winterborne, modest planter of trees and presser and seller of cider from the apple orchards. Giles is himself the object of a hopeless passion on the part of Marty South, a poor girl of the neighborhood who often helps him in his planting.

At first her father favors Grace's union with Giles; but when he sees the great transformation wrought in her by her schooling, he begins to regret the spending of so much money upon her only that she may sink back again to their own social level. And when, by the death of an old man, upon whose life depended Giles's title to certain land, the woodlander becomes a man without property, Melbury uses all his influence with his daughter in favor of her more promising suitor. In the meantime Grace herself has been somewhat offended in her cultivated tastes by the awkwardness and social inexperience of her rustic lover. And she is brought gradually and reluctantly to a marriage with Fitzpiers.

She soon comes to realize that she cannot live up to his standards of social aloofness, that she entertains a fondness for rustic persons and manners which her gentleman husband disdains. And Fitzpiers, falling in love with a lady of ardent temperament who occupies the manor house of Hintock, takes advantage of his profession of doctor to carry on a love affair suitable to the standards of smart society. In the end he goes abroad to live with his Mrs. Charmond; and the remorseful timber merchant busies himself to get a divorce for his abused daughter so that she may marry her honest and devoted woodland lover. Before this can be accomplished—and indeed it was not, we know, possible of accomplishment—Mrs. Charmond has been murdered by another jealous lover, and Fitzpiers comes home to his wife.

But by this time her disgust for him and her love for Giles have gathered strength; and upon the return of her husband, she takes flight into the forest, to Giles in his little hut. There the chivalrous man turns out of his home to give her shelter, though he is suffering himself with fever; and as a result of lying in a leaky lean-to, he becomes mortally sick. When Grace finally realizes his condition, she takes him into the cottage and summons the doctor. The doctor is her husband, and the situation is a strange one. It is made the stranger by her proud perverse declaration to Fitzpiers that she has been, in the full sense of the word, the lover of Giles.

After the death of Giles, it is but a matter of time and favoring circumstance till husband and wife make their explanations, and come together again for life with chastened passions and a will to conformity.

But the last word is for Giles; and it is spoken by Marty South, the other pure and unmixed type of the poetry of the woods and of the humble life. For many months, ever since the death of Giles, she and Grace had come once a week by night to lay flowers on his grave. But now Grace has failed her in their tryst, and she alone is faithful to the man they had both loved. So there in the moonlight she stoops above the grave, a slight girlish figure, and talks in whispers to the dead man:

> "Now, my own, own love, you are mine, and on'y mine; for she has forgot 'ee at last, although for her you died. But I— whenever I get up I'll think of 'ee. Whenever I plant the young larches I'll think that none can plant as you planted; and whenever I split a gad, and whenever I turn the cider-wring, I'll say none could do it like you. If ever I forget your name, let me forget home and Heaven!—But no, no, my love, I never can forget 'ee; for you was a *good* man, and did good things."

2

This is poetry. And everything that is finest in the book is poetry. It lies in the special charm of this district, rendered with such affectionate penetration, a district which must be more like what Mr. Hardy knew as a child than any other kind of country of which he has given account in his variegated Wessex. Even more than Egdon Heath or the Greenwood Tree, this is a region "outside the gates of the world"; and the dweller in towns who makes his way hither must leave the forsaken coach road where the trees "make the way-side hedges ragged with their drip and shade," to follow an even more secluded lane into the heart of the woodland. We have not here the pastures and grain fields of *The Madding Crowd* and *Tess*. Here we have the vegetable world not so much dominated by, as dominating, man. It is a place where men nestle like birds under the heavy thatch of horizontal branches, where the sun is not seen complete till mid-day, and the rain drips long from the fringe of boughs upon the garden plots, where men in motion are seen with "leaf-shadows running their quick succession over their forms." The most open country here is that of the orchards, ancient apple trees, dappling the ground with shadow. But we are more likely to find ourselves among the mossed and fungused ashes and elms of the sunless forest, or "amid beeches under which nothing grew," their leaves "rustling in the breeze with a sound almost metallic, like the sheet-iron foliage of the fabled Jarnvid wood."

Here is the reign of trees, who are like sacred beings; and Winterborne is their priest or tutelary god.   In the time of his absence,

He rose upon Grace's memory as the fruit-god and the wood-god in alternation, sometimes leafy, and smeared with green lichen, as she had seen him among the sappy boughs of the plantation; sometimes cider-stained, and with apple pips in the hair of his arms, as she had met him on his return from cider making . . . . with his vats and presses beside him.

Giles and Marty, from their long labors together, had possessed themselves of all the finer mysteries of the woods,

those remoter signs and symbols which, seen in few, were of runic obscurity, but all together made an alphabet.   From the light lashing of the twigs upon their faces, when brushing through them in the dark, they could pronounce upon the species of the tree whence they stretched; from the quality of the wind's murmur through a bough they could in like manner name its sort afar off.

There was even a mystic sympathy between the trees and Winterborne by virtue of which he could make them grow better than other men.

And it was by a wonderful stroke of the poetical imagination that the author made the destiny of his woodland minister depend upon the life of a tree.   In the beginning of the story Winterborne is the owner of several houses with their orchards and gardens. But, by a strange inequitable arrangement, which has been elsewhere employed by Mr. Hardy in the ironic entanglement of men's fates, his ownership or lease is made to hang upon the life of another woodlander, the father of Marty South. And the sick brain of old Mr. South is possessed of a superstitious notion, not confined to Wessex or the nineteenth century, that his life is somehow bound up with that of another being, in this case, a great elm tree growing before his dwelling. It is his notion that in his youth he had in some way made an enemy of the ancient tree, and that now it threatens his life every time the wind blows. So rooted is his obsession that to the doctor it seems that the tree is actually frightening the old man to death; and he orders it felled to save his patient's life. It is Winterborne who cuts it down. But instead of saving his life, the disappearance of the tree actually paralyzes the sick man with amazement, and he dies on the same day as the sun goes down, like some fabled hero whose life continues only with the flaming of a torch or the flourishing of a flower.[1] And with the death of the old man, the young man loses possession of all his houses and lands, and so of his prospective bride—his fate, too, being determined by the dumb decree of the woodland creature whose life he had himself cut short.

3

It will be seen how beautifully the theme has been developed and bodied forth on the side of poetry. But the author was bent himself on its employment for the

[1] Perhaps Hardy, who was a reader of Shelley, remembered the death of the poet in *Alastor*, exactly as the sun went down.

purposes of drama. It is at the very start that he reminds us of the dramatic possibilities of·his woodland scene: "one of those sequestered spots outside the gates of the world . . . . where, from time to time, no less than in other places, dramas of a grandeur and unity truly Sophoclean are enacted in the real, by virtue of the concentrated passions and closely knit interdependence of the lives therein."

If this is taken for the author's account of the action that is to follow, the reader will be sorely disappointed, so far does the drama of Grace Melbury fall short of Sophoclean unity and grandeur. One reason for this at once occurs to the reader. It is the want of those concentrated passions that give their grandeur to Sophoclean tragedy, as they do to the tragedy of Eustacia Vye, of Jude the Obscure. Edgar Fitzpiers and Felice Charmond are persons of weak character and voluptuous imagination, who suffer themselves and cause pain to others. And the woman pays indeed the penalty of coquetry and volatility. But in neither case are we given the impression of a large and deep nature capable of the stirring of a grand passion. The woman is an idle sentimentalist; the man a fanciful Platonist, a sensualist, and a snob.

Much more serious and deeper rooted are the sentiments of Grace and Giles; but they are truly sentiments rather than passions, and however lovely they may be in their delicate woodland fragrance, they are not of force to break through barriers with the imperious rush of passion. Grace is too easily persuaded to marry the man she does not love to give us at that stage of the story even the impression of strong character. After the death of her lover, she is too easily persuaded to go back to her husband to give us the impression of deep feeling. Her flight to the woods on the return of Fitzpiers was not an assertion of passion for Giles; this was "the Daphnean instinct, exceptionally strong in her as a girl . . . . not lessened by . . . . her regard for another man." She did not seek out Giles as a lover, but as a trusted friend; he would help her to make her way to a schoolmate in a distant town. And it was the accident of the storm which compelled her to occupy the lone cottage, and led to her presence at the death of Giles.

It was an exciting moment when she took flight, and another when she had to summon her husband to the bedside of the man she loved. But exciting moments do not together make up drama. There was one more truly dramatic occasion earlier, when Giles, knowing already that she could not be legally separated from Fitzpiers, that she could not be his own, yet broke through all the restraints of his primitive chastity, and allowed himself that momentary embrace which Grace believed to be innocent. But several dramatic occasions in the course of a story are far from making up drama of Sophoclean unity and grandeur. Passions must be not merely "concentrated" upon a single object; they must be shown in concentration, in continuous action, to give rise to drama.

4

This is the great failure of *The Woodlanders*, as it was of *Casterbridge*, a failure in technique, the want of concentration, of continuous dramatic action. It is shown on the surface of both novels by the want of that division into parts which gave *The Native* an exterior resemblance to drama, and signalized the thoughtful massing of the subject-matter. And with no separation of parts, there can be no use of dramatic headings for the main divisions—no "Fascination," no "Closed Door." The author does not even take advantage of the division into chapters to attach significant titles to them. There is little promise of dramatic form; and the performance is not greater than the promise. The unities of place and time are less regarded than in *The Native*, especially the latter. The action of *The Woodlanders* covers three whole years, and is about evenly distributed over the whole of that time.

And instead of being developed in a small number of scenes in which there can be an acceleration and growing weight of interest, the action is dispersed through a great number of separate occasions, each one very briefly treated and dismissed. The ingenuity of the author is taxed to the utmost to provide phrases to denote transition from one place to another, from one point of time to another. "Meanwhile, in the wood they had come from"; "it chanced a few minutes before this time"; "at the same hour, and almost at the same minute, there was a conversation about Winterborne in progress in the village street"; "later in the evening"; "the next morning at breakfast"; "often during the previous night"—so they follow one another in quick succession, often within the chapter, as the author goes forward or backward, to add some new item or take up some dropped thread of the story. Often the transition is made, and often within the chapter, with no phrase of warning, and the new picture takes the place of the old with disconcerting suddenness. The author is forever telling us, too, of the change of seasons which carry the story along with them: "Spring weather came on suddenly"; "The leaves over Hintock grew denser in their substance"; "It was the beginning of June, and the cuckoo . . . ."; "The leaves overhead were now in their latter green. . . . . Summer was ending."

These indications, again, occur as often as not within the chapter, thus signalizing the progress from one stage of the story to another without even the formal starting of a new division in the narrative. It is sometimes very hard to see upon what principle the division of chapters is made. A large number of consecutive scenes are grouped together, with little regard to the period of time included, scenes in which the place and the actors are constantly changing, and which are cut off, it might almost seem, simply after a certain average of pages has been covered.

No hint is given that the author has ever taken into account any principle in regard to the point of view from which the story is to be told. In a general way, as in all fiction, we see and know and are concerned about what the main actor sees and knows and is concerned about. But numberless are the exceptions to this rule. Often we cannot be sure for more than a few sentences as to who *is* the main actor; and even within these limits we may have something presented from the point of view of a different person, or from that of the community as a whole. And then we are constantly passing, it may be within the sentence, from what a person thinks and sees on a particular occasion to a general statement in regard to his character, or human nature in general, or to some truth or circumstance known only to the omniscient manipulator of puppets. The reader is given no chance to follow for any length of time with growing interest the mental or emotional experience of a given character, his particular adventure. The center of interest is constantly shifting, and the picture is correspondingly blurred and indistinct.

Dialogue is constantly in use at all points in the story. But the passages of dialogue are very short, and constantly interspersed with description and with the narrative of action and event. Just as the reader is getting a relish for the words of men's mouths, they fall silent, and he is whisked away to be witness of the deeds of their hands, or to view the landscape in which they appear. Very seldom is a dialogue given entire; and very often the author, as if in haste to get on with his story, gives us the gist of the talk in his own words. The same baffling method is applied to action, whether upon a particular occasion or over a period of time—it is given in arid summary. There are so many things to be told, so many little happenings to be recorded, so many little explosions into speech. There are so many threads of interest to be woven into the pattern. The goal is so far off, and we must not linger by the way.

5

Let us take as a specimen the fifteenth chapter, which relates what follows upon the death of old Mr. South. We are first presented with Mr. Melbury and his perturbation over the probable loss of property by Winterborne. "When Melbury heard what had happened he seemed much moved, and walked thoughtfully about the premises. . . . . He was quite angry with circumstances for so heedlessly inflicting on Giles a second trouble when the needful one inflicted by himself was all that the proper order of events demanded." He exclaims over the situation to his daughter; but he gives her to understand all the same that Giles cannot be thought of as a son-in-law. Then we have a sudden shift to the point of view of Grace as observed by the author, who knows the secrets of her heart. "At that very moment the impracticability to which poor Winterborne's suit had been reduced was touching Grace's heart to a warmer sentiment on his behalf than she had felt for years concerning him."

And then at once, after less than a page, we turn to a new scene altogether. Giles, "meanwhile, was sitting down alone in the old familiar house which had ceased to be his, taking a calm if somewhat dismal survey of affairs." He examines the legal documents bearing upon his ownership and realizes that, whatever in fairness may be his right to the property, his legal claim depends upon the mere caprice of a woman whom he has offended. Three short paragraphs, and then a new scene. "While he was sitting and thinking a step came to the door, and Melbury appeared, looking very sorry for his position." Melbury urges him to write to Mrs. Charmond and throw himself upon her generosity. "'I would rather not,' murmured Giles. 'But you must,' said Melbury. In short he argued so cogently that Giles allowed himself to be persuaded," says the chronicler, summarizing the debate; and then, summarizing the action that followed, "the letter to

Mrs. Charmond was written and sent to Hintock House." The following paragraph shows us Melbury going home content with his good act, and Giles left alone in suspense; as well as bringing in what villagers thought about the matter.

The next three pages give us a glimpse of Marty South on the nights preceding the burial of her father, and dispose of the burial of South and the arrival of Mrs. Charmond's letter, together with the views of Winterborne, Melbury, Grace, and the countrymen upon the subject.

The rest of the chapter is a huddled record in three pages more of circumstances which, by mere chance, determine the fates of Grace and Giles. In the evening Giles discovers on the front of his house a scribbled rime to the following effect:

> "O Giles, you've lost your dwelling-place,
>   And therefore Giles, you'll lose your Grace."

Thereupon he writes a note to Melbury, giving up his claim to his daughter, takes it to the timber dealer's house, and thrusts it under the door (all this in three paragraphs). Melbury gets up in the morning and reads the note (one paragraph). In the early morning, Grace passes by Giles's house, sees the inscription, rubs out the word "lose," and substitutes the word "keep." She believes she is seen by Giles, and that he can draw the inference that she is still his (one paragraph). A paragraph is devoted to Grace's feelings. At breakfast her father shows her the letter from Giles, and she thinks her fate is sealed. Then follows nearly a page of dialogue between Giles and Marty South—it was she who had inscribed the rhyme—the upshot being that the change in the verse leaves it without sense, and that probably it was some idle boy that made it. The results for the two young people are very briefly summed up in a final paragraph—how Giles "retired into the background of human life and action thereabout," and how "Grace, thinking that Winterborne saw her write, made no further sign, and the frail bark of fidelity that she had thus timidly launched was stranded and lost."

6

It will be realized what an ineffectual patchwork is here offered to a reader eager for the excitement of a well-told story, for the intellectual stimulus of a thoughtful study, or the aesthetic gratification of a dramatic scene adequately presented. There are three main persons in whose interest the events might have been recorded, and the reader's concern thoroughly aroused by following throughout the chapter the feelings of any one of them. But instead, the interest is divided about equally among the three, Giles, Grace, and Melbury; and the reader's sympathy is dissipated still farther by his having his attention drawn to the feelings and affairs of Fitzpiers and Marty South, not to speak of the villagers *en masse*. There are three main events to any one of which the whole of a chapter might well have been devoted in order to develop its latent possibilities of suspense, of dramatic strain, of the display of character. One is the long-waited arrival of the letter which determined for Giles whether he was rich or poor; the second is the scene between him and Melbury in which the latter announces his attitude toward the former's suit; the third is the alteration of the scribbled verse and the circumstances by which it fails to carry its message to Giles. As a matter of fact, in each case there is a languid and feeble attempt to do justice to the particular event, soon dropped as if from weariness, want of resource, or a fatal compulsion to hurry on. "Eleven times had Winterborne gone to that corner of the ride, and looked up its long straight slope through the wet grays of winter dawn. . . . . On the twelfth day the man of missives, while yet in the extreme distance, held up his hand, and Winterborne saw a letter in it." Such is the tribute paid by the author to the convention of suspense aroused by successive disappointments.

It is in similar ineffectual fashion that, in a later chapter, he tries to make us feel the fatal passing of the days that lead to the unhappy marriage of Grace. "The interim closed up its perspective surely and silently. . . . . Day after day waxed and waned. . . . . The narrow interval that stood before the day diminished yet. . . . . The day loomed so big and nigh that her prophetic ear. . . . . She awoke: the morning had come. Five hours later she was the wife of Fitzpiers." These are the rustiest springs of ancient melodrama, the sorriest apology for a story not told!

As for the strong potential scene between Melbury and Giles, only the opening remarks are given, and the author shies at the critical point like a horse shying at a fence too high for him. The alteration of the verse by Grace and the writing and delivery of the letter from Giles were presumably accompanied by lively feelings on her side and on his; but the nearest we come to an adequate presentation of anything concerned with this matter is the bit of dialogue between Giles and Marty, as the briefly recorded result of which, "Winterborne said no more, and dismissed the matter from his mind."

There is evidently no attempt to distinguish between major and minor incident, between significant and non-significant point of view, no attempt to select for presentation those scenes which are capable of being presented with effectiveness, that point of view which shall do most for enlightening the reader or working on his sympathies. Everything is of equal importance; every event is brought on the scene to be dismissed before its effect is produced. There seems to be no notion of that *scenic* art, that art of *representation*, which was the constant preoccupation of Stevenson and Henry James, and which has been sedulously cultivated by their successors, by Mr. Conrad, and Mr. Walpole and Mrs. Wharton. The *facts* are given, to be sure; and so given as to suggest that it is the sole concern of the author to inform us of the facts—to get them in the record, like entries in some ancient chronicle. But more often than not, they are facts for the understanding merely, and by no means pictures for the imagination. We know them to be facts; but we do not realize them, are not convinced by them, have not taken them into our hearts.

7

We are frequently reminded throughout this book of Mr. Hardy's extreme fondness for facts. A fact is always gold to him; and it makes little difference whether it is rough in the ore, and mingled with worthless matter, or whether it has been separated and stamped with the king's stamp. Without the aid of ponderable facts he seems to be helpless and without resource; there is something touching about the way he leans upon them, his naïve faith that in them salvation is to be found.

Such, in *The Woodlanders*, are the circumstances leading to the death of Felice Charmond. That she should die is in itself not necessary to the reunion of Grace and Fitzpiers; still less the complicated machinery by which her death is brought about. Altogether disproportionate in the story is the attention given to Marty South's sale of her hair to Mrs. Charmond; and in the end it serves no purpose but to motivate the separation of Felice and Fitzpiers, which might so much better have been motivated—without machinery—by the natural decay of a selfish and sentimental love. Charmingly naïve and characteristic is the impulse of Marty to serve Grace by revealing to Fitzpiers that his mistress' hair is not her own. But crude enough is the obtrusion upon the strictly sentimental problem of Fitzpiers and Grace of this hard, unassimilated bit of information about the lovers' quarrel which grew out of Marty's letter. Still cruder and more in the line of melodrama is the intrusion of that mysterious gentleman whose jealous passion was the death of Mrs. Charmond. And one is perhaps the more amazed upon considering the deliberate forethought with which a cunning fabricator of plots has made his "plant" in the early stages of the story. There, in the midst of pertinent matter, we stumble upon a chapter introducing "a short stout man in evening-dress, carrying on one arm a light overcoat and also his hat." He had walked over from the hotel at Sherton and was seeking the lady of Hintock House. When he arrived at her home past midnight and found she was not there, he swore bitterly, it was observed, and "sighed three times before he swore." Winterborne, who had directed him upon his way, had asked him who he was, and he had replied in that compact, business-like style so often found in the speech of characters whom Hardy wants to dispose of briefly: "I am an Italianized American, a South Carolinian by birth. I left my native country on the failure of the Southern cause, and have never returned to it since." This pitiful lay figure never puts his nose into the story again except to account, in such huddled and belated fashion, for the altogether unnecessary demise of Felice Charmond. How different from that other Europeanized American and South Carolinian by birth who makes so effective an entrance and so indispensable a figure in the pattern of *The Arrow of Gold*, and who describes himself so proudly and succinctly as *"Américain, catholique, et gentilhomme"*!

Another unnecessary character is Suke Damson, the vulgar mistress of Fitzpiers before his marriage. The author doubtless felt he needed her to interpose a difficulty between Grace and her suitor. What he wants to make us feel is the qualified reluctance with which she turns from her rustic lover to the cultivated man of the world whom her father has chosen; what he offers is a poor bit of suspense over a question of facts, which does delay the marriage for the space of one chapter. It is about equally unsatisfactory as development of theme and as story-telling pure and simple.

The critical reader never ceases to wonder at the disparity between such a triumph of art as *The Native* and such bungled narrative as *The Woodlanders*. He recognizes indeed in the latter the characteristic pre-occupation of this author with matter of fact. But he cannot understand how, when he had once invented or stumbled upon the method of significant drama, he could so relapse to the no-method of rambling chronicle.

PART THREE: ART AND CRAFT AT ONE

VIII. PITY

And now, from amid the tangle of themes bizarre
and the bewildering complexity of orchestration, rises,
unannounced, a voice so simple and pure that the
hearer sits up in wonder and delight. The mind, re-
lieved of the strain of a music overlabored, goes out
eagerly to greet this theme so clear, so full, so delicately curved, and so masterfully simple in its movement. We had supposed that, in *The Return of the
Native*, our author had come as near as one could
ever hope to the abandonment of all factitious contrivance for complication of plot; that there he had
grouped his characters so cunningly, in a series of figures
circling about a single dramatic situation, as to satisfy
our utmost craving for significant unity of design.
And we were not wrong in our supposition. But now
we learn that such a dramatic pattern may in itself, by
contrast, have somewhat the effect of artifice. The
very ingenuity with which the dramatic balance is
created and maintained, the very artistry shown in
the grouping of the half-dozen players and the steady
conduct of their story to its destined catastrophe, is a
sort of contrivance. It is structural art of the highest
power, an art concealing art; and as such it excites our
admiration and our wonder. It is the perfection of its
kind, and a great achievement in novelistic technique.
It is only when we turn to the greater work succeeding
that we are reminded of the possibility of a further
refinement in the art of story-telling, of still another

kind of art, making an even stronger appeal, in which the author can do without even this legitimate measure of contrivance.

I

The story of *Tess* is one of extreme simplicity. A beautiful country girl, Tess Durbeyfield, or D'Urberville, becomes the victim of a young gentleman, her employer, Alec D'Urberville, to whom she resorts in the hope of helping her poverty-stricken family. She returns to her home, and becomes a mother; but her child does not live, and she eventually takes heart to begin life anew. She obtains employment as milker in a great dairy, and there she meets another young gentleman of fine character, Angel Clare, who is learning the business of a farmer. They fall in love; and in spite of her conviction that she is unworthy to marry, she is persuaded to engage herself to him. She makes a great effort to inform him of her past experience, but finally yields to the temptation to let it go until their marriage night. She is then encouraged to tell her secret by his volunteering a similar confession. But in spite of his generally liberal views, he cannot overcome his prejudice against a "ruined woman"; he leaves his wife, and goes to South America. Tess leads a life of great hardship; meets her old lover; and finally, in order to save her family from starvation, and persuaded that Angel will never return, consents to become Alec's mistress. Angel does come back, and finds her living with Alec. In her tragic distress she kills her seducer. She and Angel go into hiding for a time in the New Forest, but are soon taken by the police; and Tess is duly made to pay the penalty of her murder.

Simplicity unique in the novels of Hardy!

In the finer stories of the middle period, if the plots are graphically represented by a figure showing the relation of the half-dozen major characters, it will be seen how closely they are all bound together by attractions and rivalries, each one linked to every other one at least indirectly in the tangle and balance of interests resulting. Thus:

THE RETURN OF THE NATIVE

Wildeve—Eustacia—Clym

Thomasin————Mrs. Yeobright

Venn

THE MAYOR OF CASTERBRIDGE

Susan—Henchard—Lucetta

Elizabeth————Farfrae

Newson

THE WOODLANDERS

Grace—Fitzpiers—Mrs. Charmond

Giles—Melbury

Marty

When we undertake to figure *Tess* in this way,[1] we find that there are but three characters to be charted, and that it is impossible to put together even these three in a single chart without giving a misleading impression of their relations. There was never any true rivalry between Alec D'Urberville and Angel Clare, since, with the exception of one evening, which claims two chapters of the last book, the two men were never brought together in the history of Tess. The first book is exclusively the record of Tess's snaring by Alec; the third, fourth, and fifth books are taken up with the loves of Tess and Angel, with Alec entirely out of it; the sixth book relates the second pursuit by Alec, with Angel in South America. The last book belongs again to Tess and Angel, to their final love song under the shadow of death. So that a true representation of the plot can only be made in a *series* of charts, in which the successive stages of the story are shown as involving the relation in each case of but two persons.

1. (Book I)	Tess——Alec
2. (III–V)	Tess——Angel
3. (VI)	Tess——Alec
4. (VII)	Tess——Angel

How simple a plot-pattern this is may be indicated by making a similar chart for the successive moments (or books) in the story of *The Native*. In no case are there fewer than three major characters grouped in the situation of the moment. Almost every book finds a new character in the central position, between others

[1] Diagrams of this character were used by Professor H. C. Duffin, in his *Thomas Hardy: a Study of the Wessex Novels*, with the object of showing the prominence of love-affairs in Hardy's plots.

who exert a pull in opposite directions. It is a closely woven pattern of many diverse threads—an elaborate study in counterpoint. In the later book, Tess is in every case one of two characters only whose relations are the theme of the moment. It is a pattern as open as that of the simplest folk-tune.

    I. Thomasin—Wildeve—Eustacia
       Venn Mrs. Yeobright

   II. Wildeve—Eustacia—Clym
      Thomasin

 III. Eustacia—Clym—Mrs. Yeobright

  IV. Wildeve—Eustacia—Clym
      Mrs. Yeobright

   V. Wildeve—Eustacia—Clym

The same openness of pattern appears in the setting and the chronology. In *Tess*, the setting sympathizes with the action, the place and season changing with the fortunes of the heroine. And it is not without pre-meditation that the growing passion of Tess and Angel is set in the summer foisoning of the rich dairy country, that the woman is made to "pay" in the wintry bitter-ness of a hard and cruel district, that it is among the ancient and awesome monuments of Stonehenge that the law steps in to put an end to their brief clouded romance. All this is not without premeditation, not without a great refinement of art. But this is the usual course of a story—a ballad or a tale—flowing like a stream through changing country, with the natural vicissitudes of landscape. And it actually puts less strain upon the reader's attention than a design, like that of *The Native*, in which all threads of plot are made to cross in one place, beneath one sky and within the limits of one fixed horizon. It gives less the *impression* of design, or contrivance.

And the same thing is true of the greater extension in time allowed to the story of Tess. The events leading to her seduction are made to cover one summer; and it is not until two years later, after a time of retirement with her disgrace, that Tess goes forth again to battle with life and to hope. All summer is given to the growth of her love for Angel, and it is not till New Year's that they are married. There follows the bitter winter of their separation, and then their brief reunion in the spring; so that the arrest and execution of Tess takes place fully three years after she first started out from Marlott to seek her fortune in the world. This is not an arrangement suitable to a drama, in which the lines of many lives, long converging, are to be shown at the point where at last they cross and tangle. But it does seem more like life: life that holds its issues in abeyance; life so full of seeming conclusions and new starts; life that, when it once conceives a grudge against one of its creatures, loves so to play at cat and mouse with him— to let him go and then catch him again, leaving time for recovery between one seizure and the next.

It is not drama now that Hardy wants, but pathos.
It is not the conflict of wills among antagonists chosen
for their strength. It is the struggle of weakness and
innocence in the clutch of circumstance. And this
accounts for the transcendent appeal of the story of
Tess. No matter how much we may admire the
cunning workmanship of the earlier novel, no matter how
breathlessly we may have followed the march of destiny
in the story of Eustacia Vye, embracing in our concern
the desperate nostalgia of Eustacia, the jealous mother-
liness of Mrs. Yeobright, the unworldly aspirations of
Clym—we cannot feel for any of these the simple love
and grief that Tess inspires; no fates of theirs can make
us so cry out against the cruelty of life. It may be an
irony hard for the artist to stomach. Not all his
originality of conception, not all the devices of structural
art, not all the resources of his wisdom and science
avail him so well with the mass of his readers as the
direct appeal of one heart to another.

I do not wish to imply that *Tess* is in any way inferior
in art to *The Native*. But it is an art supremely free
from self-consciousness, and making the reader uncom-
monly at ease. And quite irrespective of the degree of
art displayed, the fact remains—let it be palatable or
unpalatable to artist or critic—that the greatest element
of appeal in *Tess* is the pathos inherent in its story, and
after that the heat of feeling with which the author
traces the sufferings of his heroine. And it is this
pathos, and this heat of feeling—voicing itself in accents
of great beauty—that make the superiority of *Tess*,
I will not say merely to *The Native*, but to any other
English novel of its period.

2

Not but what the story of Tess has its elements of drama, its long passages of tension about a joined issue. There is one series of chapters devoted to a steady progressive action, leading to a dramatic climax, the continuous development of a single situation, absolutely without interruption, longer than anything of the sort in any novel of Hardy's. This includes the third and fourth books and the early chapters of the fifth, and covers the whole history of Angel and Tess from her arrival at Talbothays to their separation after the bitter honeymoon.

The third book is wholly devoted to the leisurely record of their growing love. It is here that Mr. Hardy has taken time for once to do full justice to his story, to give a complete representation of a process instead of indicating it in cramped and huddled shorthand. The result is that we are given the completest sense of the reality of these lovers and their passion, we are charmed with the fresh and flower-like beauty of its unfolding, and we are touched with awe by its steady progress "under the force of irresistible law." There is no more hurry than in the accompanying progress of the seasons from May to midsummer, and from midsummer to the dog days; and no more likelihood of retardation or reversal of the process.

It is with little flourish that Angel is first introduced in the cow-barton, commenting (scholar-like) on the medieval character of the dairyman's anecdote, and occasionally "uttering a private ejaculation" (gentleman-like) over the hardness of the milking. The next impression Tess receives of his character is through his ranging the cows so as to give her the easier ones. And then comes the soundless June evening, and their slight exchange of sentiments on the fearsomeness of "life in general," when each wonders that the other "should look upon it as a mishap to be alive"—he "a man of clerical family and good education, and above physical want," and she "but a milkmaid." "They were mutually puzzled at what each revealed, and awaited new knowledge of each other's character and moods. . . . . Every day, every hour, brought to him one more little stroke of her nature, and to her one more of his."

They could not help meeting; and somewhat weird and out of the ordinary were the conditions under which they met, making for a kind of breathless suspension on the edge of passion, and for a strangely ideal representation of one another.

They met daily in that strange and solemn interval of time, the twilight of the morning, in the violet or pink dawn; for it was necessary to rise early, so very early here. . . . .

Being so often—perhaps not always by chance—the first two persons to get up at the dairy-house, they seemed to themselves the first persons up of all the world. . . . . The spectral, half-compounded, aqueous light which pervaded the open mead impressed them with a feeling of isolation, as if they were Adam and Eve. At this dim, inceptive stage of the day, Tess seemed to Clare to exhibit a dignified largeness, both of disposition and physique, and almost regnant power. . . . .

The mixed, singular, luminous gloom in which they walked along together to the spot where the cows lay often made him think of the Resurrection hour. He little thought that the Magdalen might be at his side. Whilst all the landscape was in neutral shade, his companion's face, which was the focus of his eyes, rising above the mist stratum, seemed to have a sort of phosphorescence upon it. She looked ghostly, as if she were

merely a soul at large. In reality her face, without appearing to
do so, had caught the cold gleam of day from the northeast;
his own face, though he did not think of it, wore the same aspect
to her.

It was then, as has been said, that she impressed him most
deeply. She was no longer the milkmaid, but a visionary essence
of woman—a whole sex condensed into one typical form. He
called her Artemis, Demeter, and other fanciful names, half-
teasingly, which she did not like because she did not understand
them.

"Call me Tess," she would say, askance; and he did.

Then it would grow lighter, and her features would become
simply feminine; they had changed from those of a divinity
who could confer bliss to those of a being who craved it.[1]

Thus far there has been no dramatic tension, since
no issue has arisen. But a very critical issue is poten-
tially present in Tess's determination, taken on her
second setting out in the world, that she would never
allow a man to marry her and her past. And the issue
is brought to the fore by two slight incidents: the humorous anecdote of Dairyman Crick about the girl seduced by
Jack Dollop, which revives the sense of her unworthiness,
and the overheard talk of the three milkmaids all in
love with Angel. From this time on, life is for Tess a
continual battle. She determines not to be a rival to
the other girls. Clare, on his side, is determined not
to take any unfair advantage of his position, to act with
due deliberation and regard for the woman of his love.
And then comes the heat and stagnancy of August to
bring to fruition both vegetable and human loves.
There comes the afternoon when they were milking
in the meads for coolness, and Clare, from under his

[1] Pp. 145–47.

cow, watching the tranced beauty of her profile, felt a
stimulus "like an annunciation from the sky."

Resolutions, reticences, prudences, fears, fell back like a
defeated battalion. He jumped up from his seat, and, leaving
his pail to be kicked over if the milcher had such a mind, went
quickly towards the desire of his eyes, and, kneeling down beside
her, clasped her in his arms. . . . . Tess was taken completely
by surprise, and she yielded to his embrace with unreflecting
inevitableness. Having seen that it was really her lover who had
advanced, and no one else, her lips parted, and she sank upon him
in her momentary joy, with something very like an ecstatic cry.

But this is only the beginning of the struggle for
Tess. Angel is too conscientious, even now, to take
advantage of her momentary yielding, and he does not
kiss her. It is not until his return from a visit to his
parents that he asks her to be his wife. She can find no
better reason for refusing than the probable disapproval
of his father and mother, though she hints at "experiences" which she ought to let him know. Angel makes
light of her "experiences"; but he does want an answer,
a reason. More than once she puts off her explanation;
and when at last it cannot be put off again, she falls
back on the very lame reason of her D'Urberville
descent. She is really come, she tells him, of an old
family, "all gone to nothing," and she has been told that
he "hated old families." "At the last moment her
courage had failed her, she feared his blame for not
telling him sooner; and her instinct of self-preservation
was stronger than her candor."

The struggle proceeds from this moment of failing
courage through its harrowing stages of intensification.
Having at last acknowledged her love for Angel, Tess

now desperately appeals to her mother for advice; and her mother advises, nay conjures and commands her not to let anyone know her secret, reminding her of a promise to that effect made by Tess on her leaving home. And thus "steadied by a command from the only person in the world who had any shadow of right to control her action, Tess grew calm." She contents her conscience with putting off the date of the wedding. But that will not serve for long; and at last,

> The word had been given; the number of the day written down. Her naturally bright intelligence had begun to admit the fatalistic convictions common to field-folk and those who associate more extensively with natural phenomena than their fellow-creatures; and she accordingly drifted into that passive responsiveness to all things her lover suggested, characteristic of the frame of mind.

But she was not wholly pacified in spirit. She wrote again vainly to her mother. When her wedding gown arrived, she remembered the ballad of the guilty Queen, and she thought: "Suppose this robe should betray her condition by its changing color, as her robe had betrayed Queen Guénever."

Then comes the visit to a neighboring town where Tess is recognized by a man from Trantridge, the scene of her affair with Alec. The man, upon receiving a blow from Angel, hastens to declare that he is mistaken, and Angel thinks nothing more of the matter. But Tess is once more aroused to the need of action, and she makes her attempt to reach him with her written confession. It is not till the wedding morning that she discovers the missing note where it has lain unobserved under the edge of the carpet; and then she makes one

more effort, in their brief moment on the landing, to
tell him of her "faults and blunders." But her courage
so naturally melts away under his urgency!—let them not
spoil the day with confession of faults, but leave them
till they are settled in their house.

And so the day passes swiftly with its activities and
ill omens, the knot is tied fast, and they find themselves
in the evening alone before the fire. Her way is made
easier by Angel's confession, and at last she summons
strength to tell her story straight.

But we are still to be held in suspense through the
terrible days and nights while Angel is making up his
mind. We have hopes that he will be moved by the
humility and the manifest loveliness of her character;
that her suggestion of a divorce, though made in ignorance of the law, will convince him of her nobility; that
his sleep-walking tenderness is a sign of relenting.
And we are not released from our suspense until we read:
"When Tess had passed over the crest of the hill he
turned to go his own way, and did not know that he
loved her still."

3

So ends that part of the story which recounts the
growing loves of Tess and Angel, their marriage and
separation. It is the heart of the story, and what
gives dramatic force to the whole narrative, having
made us for good and all hot champions of Tess and
sorely sensitive to the pathos of all her sufferings.
Technically it bears considerable resemblance to the
second and third books of *The Native*, which recount the
love-making and marriage of Eustacia and Clym. But

there are several important points of difference. The dramatic tension is not one created by conflicting wills or hopes of persons opposed to one another; it is for the most part a struggle within the breast of the heroine, in which the antagonists are Passion and Conscience. While, therefore, the reader is held in suspense, and receives a strong impression of the strain upon the will and the heart of Tess, he watches here no marshaling of interest against interest, of character against character, such as peoples the stage in *The Native*. We are not so much taken up with the play of forces as with the moral suffering of a woman in the grip of a dilemma, who cannot enjoy the supreme happiness within her reach because of an honorable scruple in regard to her past.

Moreover, this long passage of strain does not grow directly, like that of *The Native*, out of a dramatic situation already developed, nor lead directly into the dramatic climax of the story. It is the second of three major episodes in the life of the heroine: the story takes a new start with her rally from the first experience, and again with the beginning of the "payment" which leads to the "fulfilment." This is another feature of the non-dramatic, the loose-patterned or epic style of narration,[1] appropriate to a tale of suffering.

4

And, strong as may be the hold upon the reader of this central episode, the strongest scenes are yet to come. He has still before him those parts of the story where

[1] This distinction between the epic and dramatic types in Hardy's novels has been made by Mr. Lascelles Abercrombie in his *Thomas Hardy: a Critical Study*.

he can scarcely read for tears, and where he cannot
possibly read aloud for very shame of his choking voice.
For the main appeal is not to our dramatic sense, but to
our hearts. It is really so throughout the book. It is
with our hearts that we respond to the picture of the
helpless Durbeyfield children, those "half-dozen little
captives under hatches compelled to sail" with their
parents in the crazy Durbeyfield ship. It is our hearts
that contract at the killing of their horse Prince, their
breadwinner, when Tess and Abraham were driving
him to market with the beehives. More pathetic than
dramatic are indeed the scenes in which we behold Tess
awaiting the decision of Angel, after her confession.
For while we are made to feel that her case is a good one,
that there were "many effective chords which she could
have stirred by an appeal," we can but witness her
weakness and prostration of spirit in a situation she is
so helpless to control.

From this point on the pathos deepens steadily to
the end. The hardships of the winter labor in the
turnip field, the persecutions of her brutal employer,
the depressing comments of Angel's brothers, so unluckily
overheard by Tess, and that most unlucky encounter
with Alec, the convert—these follow one another so
rapidly, and yet with such convincing simplicity and
sobriety in the manner of their setting forth, that we
grow positively tremulous with emotion, ready to yield
our tears to any direct appeal. And such direct appeal
is made by the two despairing letters of Tess to Angel.
One knows not which is the more moving of the two.
First comes the long letter in which she says, "I must
cry to you in my trouble—I have no one else," a letter

of self-justification, full of intense longing, fear, and pain. "The daylight has nothing to show me, since you be not here. . . . ." And then, some time later, as she sees herself being forced back relentlessly into the power of Alec, she writes in haste those lines of passionate reproach: "O, why have you treated me so monstrously, Angel! I do not deserve it. I have thought it all over carefully, and I can never, never forgive you! . . . . I will try to forget you. It is all injustice I have received at your hands!" Here the reader's feeling of pity is mingled with exultation over the utterance for once of the bitter truth by the long-suffering woman.

But more typical, and more pathetic, is her usual spirit of tender submissiveness and hopefulness. There is the picture of her singing in the fields, perfecting the ballads that Angel had seemed to like best in their milking days. Like Clym at his furze-cutting, she would sing of "the break o' the day," only in rude English instead of elaborate and elegant French.

> Arise, arise, arise!
> And pick your love a posy,
> All of the sweetest flowers
> That in the garden grow.
> The turtle doves and small birds
> In every bough abuilding,
> So early in the spring-time,
> At the break o' the day!

It would have melted the heart of a stone to hear her singing these ditties, whenever she worked apart from the rest of the girls in this cold, hard time; the tears running down her cheeks all the while at the thought that perhaps he would not, after all, come to hear her, and the simple, silly words of the songs resounding in painful mockery of the aching heart of the singer.[1]

[1] P. 393.

We have next to follow the dreary exodus of the
Durbeyfields from their home on the death of the
father, their pilgrimage to Kingsbere, and the ironic
encampment of the homeless, poverty-stricken family
under the wall of the church within which lay the vaults
of the knightiy D'Urbervilles. Within the church Tess
has her encounter with the ubiquitous Alec, with his
sinister offers of assistance; and upon his departure,
she bends down over the entrance to the vaults with
her cry, "Why am I on the wrong side of this door?"

The next we see of Tess is in the lodgings at Sandbourne, where Angel found her living with Alec, and the
two "stood fixed, their baffled hearts looking out of their
eyes with a joylessness pitiful to see. Both seemed to
implore something to shelter them from reality." It
was very little that either could find to say on facts so
irreversible; and before we know it, the scene is over.

It is to Alec that she addresses her most passionate
words of reproach and hatred and self-justification.
This is the climax of the book; it is meant to prepare
us for the murder of Alec, and the raving words are
suited to the tongue of the most tragic of emotional
actresses. But it is not drama in the strict sense which
here holds us in thrall. It is the pathos of inexorable
fate; it is the tears in things.

". . . . And then my dear, dear husband came home to
me . . . . and I did not know it! . . . . And you had used your
cruel persuasion upon me . . . . and you would not stop using it
—no—you did not stop! My little sisters and brothers and
my mother's needs—they were the things you moved me by
. . . . and you said my husband would never come back—never;
and you taunted me, and said what a simpleton I was to expect
him. . . . . And at last I believed you and gave way! . . . .
And then he came back!"

It is to Alec that Tess addressed her words, and it is against him as an individual that she rouses her fury to the point of action. But for our part, we hardly take him into account. We are not concerned with the assignment of responsibility, the estimate of merits in the case. We have not place in our hearts for any other sentiment than compassion. Or if we are moved to rage, it is against that impersonal order which makes possible such a pitiful frustration of happiness.

There follows the brief respite of the time of hiding, and then the awesome arrival of Angel and Tess at the monstrous temple of Stonehenge. She lies down upon one of the great stones, which Angel believes to be an altar. They discuss the religious character of the place, and so she is reminded of the question of immortality. Realizing that her days on earth are numbered, she wants to know if Angel thinks they will meet again after they are dead. It is the old pitiful question of mortals striving against the conditions of their mortality, a question that recurs with such increase of pathos since the low tide of Christian faith, in our present days of dubiety. But never can it have been put under more affecting conditions than here by this murderess about to be apprehended, this poor girl addressing her lover from whom she had been so cruelly separated, resting now a moment in the presence of these mysterious monuments whose timeless permanence so dwarfs, but cannot suppress, the hopes and aspirations of human creatures. Even at such a moment, Angel cannot bring himself to give her comfort; but she falls asleep on the rock, tired out with their long flight. And then we have the most touchingly beautiful scene, perhaps,

in all English fiction—the scene of her arrest at daybreak, and the last recorded words of these ill-starred
lovers.

Like a greater than himself, to the critical question at the
critical time he did not answer; and they were again silent.
In a minute or two her breathing became more regular, her clasp
of his hand relaxed, and she fell asleep. The band of silver pale-
ness along the east horizon made even the distant parts of the
Great Plain appear dark and near; and the whole enormous
landscape bore that impress of reserve, taciturnity, and hesitation
which is usual just before day. The eastward pillars and their
architraves stood up blackly against the light, and the great
flame-shaped Sun-stone beyond them; and the stone of sacrifice
midway. Presently the night wind died out, and the quivering
little pools in the cup-like hollows of the stones lay still. At the
same time something seemed to move on the verge of the dip
eastward—a mere dot. It was the head of a man approaching
them from the hollow beyond the Sun-stone. Clare wished they
had gone onward, but in the circumstances decided to remain
quiet. The figure came straight towards the circle of pillars in
which they were.

He heard something behind him, the brush of feet. Turning,
he saw over the prostrate column another figure; then, before
he was aware, another was at hand on the right, under a trilithon,
and another on the left. The dawn shone full on the front of
the man westward, and Clare could discern from this that he was
tall, and walked as if trained. They all closed in with evident
purpose. Her story then was true! Springing to his feet, he
looked around for a weapon, means of escape, anything. By
this time the nearest man was upon him.

"It is no use, sir," he said. "There are sixteen of us on the
Plain, and the whole country is reared."

"Let her finish her sleep!" he implored in a whisper of the men
as they gathered round.

When they saw where she lay, which they had not done till
then, they showed no objection, and stood watching her, as still
as the pillars around. He went to the stone, and bent over her,

holding one poor little hand; her breathing now was quick and small, like that of a lesser creature than a woman. All waited in the growing light, their faces and hands as if they were silvered, the remainder of their figures dark, the stones glistening a green-gray, the Plain still a mass of shade. Soon the light was strong, a ray shone upon her unconscious form, peering under her eyelids and waking her.

"What is it, Angel?" she said, starting up. "Have they come for me?"

"Yes, dearest," he said, "They have come."

"It is as it should be," she murmured. "Angel, I am almost glad—yes, glad! This happiness could not have lasted. It was too much. I have had enough; and now I shall not live for you to despise me!"

She stood up, shook herself, and went forward, neither of the men having moved.

"I am ready," she said quietly.[1]

5

This is not the pathos of a professional compeller of tears. It is the inadvertent yielding of one who looks upon weeping as an unmanly weakness, and whose effort has always been to state the painful truth in the dry style of matter of fact. It is remarkable that never once in the dozen novels which preceded *Tess* had Hardy ever offered so direct an invitation to tears, as here we meet so many times. Only once perhaps in all that earlier record of human experience does even a sensitive reader feel constrained to tears—by the last words on the subject of Clym Yeobright and his itinerant preaching. His preaching was variously received. "But everywhere *he* was kindly received, for the story of his life had become generally known." It is only then, and through those simple words, that we are made to

[1] Pp. 453-55.

feel in its full poignancy the sadness of this "story of his life." Equally simple, in general, is the pathos of Tess, as simple as her quiet words to the officers, "I am ready." ˙It is the accumulated feeling of a lifetime that overflows in this culminating work of art.

A glance at the dates may here be enlightening. Heretofore his production of novels had been extremely rapid. From *Desperate Remedies* in 1871 to *The Wood-landers* in 1887, Mr. Hardy had turned out a novel almost every year, with never more than a two-year interval. He must have been deeply immersed in the business of inventing plots and creating characters, too busy with creation, it might be thought, to have time for mature reflection. Especially from the time of *The Native* he had been pouring out novel after novel in almost feverish haste. But with the completion of *The Woodlanders* he rested from this labor for the extraordinary space of five years. One volume of tales was collected and published in the interval, and another was put forth in the same year with *Tess*. But we cannot suppose that these would demand the same long strain of thought as the construction of a novel. It is like a period of retirement. The philosopher, the student of life, has industriously collected his materials, like a Wallace or a Darwin in his voyage to the South Seas; and now he goes into his retreat to muse over what he has found and to extract its secret essence. As he allows things to fall into due perspective, many details are lost to view, many complications cease to obtrude themselves; the lines of life become more simple, and everything begins to present itself in the light of one great dominant feeling. The general beauty and pitifulness of life gather about the form and history of a certain poor girl, and all his thought and feeling on the subject of human destiny join in one flood of compassion for one typical human being.

It is the old theme of a woman's secret to be told or to be suppressed, the sort of theme which had by this time perhaps become shopworn in the great mart of paper-covered novels. And Mr. Hardy was moving, consciously or unconsciously, in that current of sentiment which makes the popularity of women novelists whose names do not often appear in the bluebooks of literature, but who make the fortunes of the publishers of Seaside (or Bertha Clay) Libraries—the "Duchesses" and Charlotte M. Braemes, who were names to conjure with long before Mr. Hardy became the subject of literary study! The pure woman, the innocent country girl, cheated or forced into a false position; the secret to be told or to be kept silent, and in any case sure to be the source of trouble and misery; a world which will not give fair trial or a second chance to a woman with a past—are not these the very stock in trade of the paper-covered novel, which still finds its passionate readers in so many kitchens and hall bedrooms? *The Wife's Secret, Beyond Pardon, A Woman's Error, One False Step, The Shadow of a Sin:* such are a few of the suggestive titles out of hundreds credited to the sole pen of one Charlotte M. Braeme, author of *Dora Thorne,* and for sale at twenty-five cents each in the eighties and nineties.

It is true that these stories seldom come out tragically, like that of Tess. It is true that the heroine is seldom permitted to be even technically in the wrong, like her.

serial

But it is significant that, in the magazine version of *Tess*, addressed to the family circle, Mr. Hardy allowed his heroine to pass for absolutely impeccable. In place of the seduction of Tess by Alec, the magazine reader was informed of a "fake" marriage by which the innocent girl was entrapped. And even in the book she appears sufficiently in the light of a victim to make sure appeal to the Saxon chivalrous instinct. And with due allowance for the insipidity called for in a paper-covered novel, one recognizes in these machine-made tales the primary elements of Hardy's great work of art.

There is no absolute divorce between "literature" proper and the literature of the dime novel. Themes which receive their crudely sentimental and melo-dramatic treatment in the one are sure to appear above the surface, somewhat refined, it may be, but recogniz-able. Meredith, when he put forth *Rhoda Fleming*, showed in his chapter headings a consciousness that he was writing somewhat in the manner of *East Lynne* or suchlike melodrama. And *Tess of the D'Urbervilles* came at a time when, in serious literature, especially in plays, a great deal of attention was being paid to the subject of the *déclassée*—the woman who would come back, the woman who lives under "the shadow of a sin," the woman who has to pay for "one false step." *The Second Mrs. Tanqueray* will suffice to suggest the currency of a theme which is treated by such other notable hands as Oscar Wilde and Henry Arthur Jones. So that Hardy's subject was timely from the point of view of the "high brow" as well as popular in the original sense of the word. And that one of his novels which is most satisfying to the critic for the beauty and seriousness of its art is at the same time the one to make, from the time of its first appearance, an appeal to the widest circle of readers.

All along, the theme of a woman's secret had appealed to the imagination of Hardy, and he had more or less nibbled at it in several novels. In his very first book there is in the background the case of Cytherea Aldclyffe, who met too late the man she should have married, but who, fearing the results of a confession, "withdrew from him by an effort and pined." His second novel rings down the curtain on his heroine thinking of "a secret she would never tell," of her brief infidelity in thought toward her lover when she came under the spell of the gentlemanly clergyman and his brilliant offers. In *The Hand of Ethelberta* and *The Mayor of Casterbridge*, it is quite a different sort of secret which is suppressed: in the one case, Ethelberta's humble status, in the other, the fact that Elizabeth-Jane is not really the daughter of Henchard. It is in *A Pair of Blue Eyes* that we find the nearest anticipation of *Tess*. For there we have the heroine similarly declaring to the leading man that she has a confession to make, similarly putting it off, and then at the last moment losing heart and confessing to something else of quite insignificant importance. But this is, after all, no very close approximation to the theme of *Tess*. It is the real seriousness of the thing to be confessed, the fact that Tess does finally make her confession instead of leaving the truth to be discovered through the revelations of some Mrs. Jethway, and the very heavy "payment" exacted, which give the latter its specific character.

It may seem strange that the author who had worked so deliberately the traditional themes and devices of the popular story-teller, one who was so clearly bent on producing something that would satisfy the public, should have been so long in taking up for serious treatment a subject the like of which had proved effective in sentimental novels without number. It was probably to a large degree his consideration for Victorian prudery that led him so long to fight shy of the subject of *Tess*. But it was also, no doubt, that grave seriousness with which, after all, he had always approached at least the subject-matter of his art. He was willing to adopt many of the conventions and the standard procedure of his trade; but he would not consent to falsify human nature if he could help it, and he would not lower himself to make a deliberate bid for tears. One is inclined to believe that, in taking up at last this hackneyed theme of the fatal secret and the "soiled dove," Mr. Hardy was by no means fully conscious how straight he was aiming at the bull's-eye of popularity. He was perhaps unaware of the wide currency of his theme; perhaps it was an infection which he took, like any simple reader, because it was in the air. He no doubt thought he was telling the story of Tess not because it was popular but because it was true. He had himself first succumbed to the pity of it, and that is why his readers so inevitably succumbed. It is, in the last analysis, because he shared to such a degree the popular psychology that he was able to score so great a popular success.

It is certainly not because of any deliberate working of the pathetic possibilities of the subject. One does not see how, short of suppression, he could have disposed more simply of the scene of Tess's execution, of the meeting of Tess and Angel at Sandbourne, or the picture of Tess singing her ballads in the wintry field. The story does not seem to be constructed so as to lead to these scenes and bring them into prominence. They rather fall as it were casually, by the way; and we pass on quickly to what follows. It is this very economy of statement, carrying with it a sense of matter of fact, that makes the passages so convincing to the intelligent reader.

There is even a kind of detachment, an almost scientific manner of statement, that might interfere with the effect of any pathos less seriously grounded, as in the way of referring to Tess and explaining her appearance during the christening of her baby. "The emotional girl" he calls her, almost as if to forbid us to take the incident sentimentally. He looks upon her more objectively than would suit the purposes of the professionally pathetic writer, showing her to us as she is seen by her brothers and sisters. "The children gazed up at her with more and more reverence, and no longer had a will for questioning. She did not look like Sissy to them now, but as a being large, towering, and awful—a divine personage with whom they had nothing in common."

In this scene the pathos is somewhat qualified, it may be, by the satirical bias with which the author regards the rite of infant baptism and the beliefs in regard to it which so tortured the girl-mother. This fear of the child's damnation is, of course, what gives its peculiar force to the act, as the doubt of immortality is what gives its poignancy to Tess's question at the end of the story. But in the earlier case, at least, there is a note of philosophic scorn in the terms in which the author refers to "poor Sorrow's campaign against sin, the world, and the devil" and to the "kind of heaven" which would be lost to him by an irregularity in his baptism, which detracts from the simplicity of feeling ordinarily going with pathos.

There is indeed a philosophic coloring to the whole narrative which denotes a degree of reflection generally fatal to pathos. These are the only terms on which this author will condescend to the moving of tears. Not content to relate the loss of Prince and the grief of the Durbeyfields, Hardy is impelled to give to the incident a wider significance by the reference to blighted stars. In their nocturnal drive, Tess has been giving little Abraham what information she commands on the subject of the stars. "They sometimes seem to be like apples on our stubbard tree. Most of them splendid and sound—a few blighted." And to his question as to what kind we live on, she replies, "A blighted one." That was before the terrible accident. Afterward, in their despair, Abraham recalls his astronomy, and asks, "'Tis because we be on a blighted star, not a sound one, isn't it, Tess?"

In the same spirit as inspired this beautiful poetic invention, Mr. Hardy is prone, less happily, to heap his scorn upon the great poets of his century for their ready faith in providence: upon the early morning optimism of Browning's Pippa; upon Wordsworth's assumption of "Nature's holy plan," and his pious sentiment about our arrival "trailing clouds of glory," in which lines, "to Tess, as to some few millions of others, there was ghastly satire."

One knows not whether to wish away or to welcome these skirmishing shots of a late-Victorian novelist disgusted with the easy optimism of early-Victorian and Georgian poets. At least they serve to guarantee the seriousness of the work, and to signalize it as of a late-Victorian order of pathos. The sufferings of Tess, at any rate, are impregnated with a moral significance which does not attach to those of Little Nell or Paul Dombey or Little Em'ly. The first two are helpless children who suffer and die, and that is pathos pure and simple. There is nothing more to be said. In the case of Little Em'ly there might have been more to be said, but the contemporaries of Dickens did not want to hear it said; and so she remained just "Little Em'ly," with no more significance than Little Nell. In Tess Durbeyfield we have a pathos of high moral significance; there is necessarily in her case a greater weight and volume of feeling. For she is a grownup woman, a responsible moral being, with intense desires, high aspirations, liable to temptation, and fearfully liable to suffering.

6

Moving as is the history of Tess in its mere incidents, it is made doubly moving by the beauty and strength of her personality. Hardy's characters are in general remarkable for their vitality; they are picked specimens of the fruit of human kind, whom we recognize as fit to represent us. But Tess is, of them all, the most full of life. With her somewhat exceptional physical endowment, she was more than usually susceptible to those sensations in which the beauty of sound and color and smell comes to us as the voice of our spirit. While Angel played his harp in the summer evening,

Tess was conscious of neither time nor space. The exaltation which she had described as being producible at will by gazing at a star, came now without any determination of hers; she undulated upon the thin notes as upon billows, and their harmonies passed like breezes through her, bringing tears into her eyes. The floating pollen seemed to be his notes made visible, and the dampness of the garden, the weeping of the garden's sensibility. Though near nightfall, the rank-smelling weed-flowers glowed as if they would not close for intentness, and the waves of color mixed with the waves of sound.

The same capacity for sensation adds intensity to all her joys and griefs, her fears and shames and hopes.

Hardy's women are—as with most novelists of his time—his most convincing and attractive characters. And Tess is the crown of all his women. Eustacia was a wonderful creation, a poetic invention, of strange exotic beauty, fit to be the wicked queen of tragedy. There is nothing of the exotic or nocturnal about our milkmaid, walking out at daybreak with her companions, or working in the harvest fields at noonday with the men and women of Marlott. She has the force of passion of Eustacia without her unscrupulous and somewhat perverse idealism. Among the earlier characters, she has more of Bathsheba than of Elfride, being a creature of the fields and barns instead of the drawing-room and the study. She is even more deeply tinctured than Bathsheba with the ocherous contact of the earth. She has a dignity of bearing like Bathsheba's; but being no independent farmer but the merest proletarian, she has more than the helplessness of her sex, and is the marked victim of an economic order that spares its Bathshebas.

She is beautiful, and real, too. For her beauty is not too perfect, and not too fully inventoried. Her eyes and mouth are the only features about which her painter is specific—her "large innocent eyes," her "large tender eyes," of indeterminate color, and her "mobile peony mouth." There is one peculiarity of her mouth upon which he dwells more than once—the way her lower lip had "of thrusting the middle of her top one upward, when they closed together after a word." It was this that was so maddening to Angel on the afternoon when he watched her at the milking till drawn to her as by an irresistible charm. Her lips were beautiful but not perfect; "and it was the touch of the imperfect upon the intended perfect that gave the sweetness, because it was that which gave the humanity." It is that which convinces us that the author was here drawing from the life. The same conviction is forced upon us by the charming colloquialism of her speech, bits of ancientry that slipped through the web of her National School training; and above all by the "stopt-diapason note which her voice acquired when her heart was in her speech, and which will never be forgotten by those who knew her." There is something in the phrasing here that makes one sure the author is speaking of an actual woman, whose voice he has heard and cannot forget.

She has every quality to make us admire her: her modesty, her sensitiveness to the disgrace of her father's drunken ways, her motherly concern for her brothers and sisters, the simple earnestness and patience with

which she performs the hard tasks imposed upon her,
and the scrupulous conscience that brings her so much
pain. Above all we find beautiful the wholeness of her
devotion to the man she loves, in its combination of
qualities traditionally distinguished as proper to woman
and to man. "Clare knew that she loved him—every
curve of her form showed that—but he did not know at
that time the full depth of her devotion, its single-
mindedness, its meekness; what long-suffering it guaran-
teed—what honesty, what endurance, what good faith."

7

This is a good woman for whom our tears are asked.
"A pure woman" he calls her in his title; an adjective
he defends in the Preface to one of the later editions.
Heretofore Mr. Hardy has been content in his novels
to make a "tacit assumption" of the conventional
standards of morality. But here, in the interest of
truth or of his story, he is impelled to interpose over
and over again his own passionate defense of his heroine's
character. He represents Tess, in the time of her
disgrace, as encompassed with

a cloud of moral hobgoblins by which she was terrified without
reason. It was they that were out of harmony with the actual
world, not she. Walking among the sleeping birds in the hedges,
watching the skipping rabbits on a moonlit warren, or standing
under a pheasant-laden bough, she looked upon herself as a
figure of Guilt intruding into the haunts of Innocence. But all the
while she was making a distinction where there was no difference.
Feeling herself in antagonism, she was quite in accord. She had
been made to break an accepted social law, but no law known to the
environment in which she fancied herself such an anomaly.

It is a very frank appeal to the law of nature from the
law of society. As expressed in the more rustic language

of Mrs. Durbeyfield, "Well, we must make the best of it, I suppose. 'Tis nater, after all, and what do please God."

But if the author is so bold in his appeal to nature, he nevertheless takes pains to clear his heroine of too much responsibility for her experience. It may be merely a social law which she had broken; but he wants us to understand that it was only through her extreme ignorance that she "had been made" to break it. It is with great feeling that Tess reproaches her mother for not telling her "there was danger in men-folk." Her fellow-workers in the fields, watching her nurse her baby, reckon that "a little more than persuading had to do wi' the coming o't. . . . . There were they that heard a sobbing one night last year in the Chase; and it mid ha' gone hard wi' a certain party if folks had come along." The circumstances of her betrayal were evidently thought out with great care so as to make her seem almost, if not quite, helpless.

It is here if anywhere in the book that we hear the creak of the machinery. Whatever he might think himself of the relative validity of the laws of nature and those of society, the author had still to reckon with his public of Saxon readers; and he must at all cost save his heroine from the slightest imputation of—well—sensuality. The trick, if such it be, was on the whole very neatly turned. It is far from the crude violence of movie and melodrama, in which the heroine is betrayed by mere force or deceit, agreeable to the Saxon persuasion—at least for purposes of romance—that no decent woman ever *can* be seduced by any other means. It is equally removed from the somewhat low-creeping

realism of George Moore; and Tess may take her place
in a higher category of character and pathos than
Esther Waters.[1] The upshot of the whole matter for
Mr. Hardy seems to be that the reproach for such an
act is in proportion to the degree of responsibility, and
that degrees of responsibility are infinite in number.

As for Tess, her responsibility is represented as
practically *nil*. She was "an almost typical woman,
but for *a slight incautiousness of character* inherited from
her race." A slight incautiousness of character, and that
inherited, can hardly amount to the *tragic fault* in a
protagonist regarded as essential to justify the ruling
powers. It would not suit the purposes of Sophocles,
of Shakespeare, of Hawthorne, or George Eliot. This
is not tragedy in the traditional sense; and the modernity
of the author is shown in his bold impiety. "'Justice'
was done," he says on recording the execution of Tess,
"and the President of the Immortals (in Aeschylean
phrase) had ended his sport with Tess." Mr. Hardy,
in his Preface, defends his exclamation against the
gods with a quotation of Gloster's words in *Lear*,

> As flies to wanton boys are we to the gods;
> They kill us for their sport.

He does not quote the words of Gloster's son,

> The gods are just, and of our pleasant vices
> Make instruments to scourge us.

More in Gloster's vein, again, is Marian's reply to
Tess's suggestion that her unhappy life is fair payment

---

[1] A recent re-reading of *Esther Waters* and other novels of Mr. Moore
leads me to doubt the justice of this statement. The greatness of
Hardy does not require the dispraise of a great contemporary.

for her own wrong-doing. "Wives are unhappy sometimes; from no fault of their husbands—from their
own," says Tess. "You've no faults, deary; that I am
sure of," is Marian's reply. "So it must be something
outside ye both." It is not immorality of which Hardy
should be accused, as he is accused, for example, by
Professor Duffin. His offense is a more modern one—
the great modern crime of impiety.

We are here concerned only with his artistic offense—
that against realism—the venial offense, when all is said,
of taking for his heroine an exceptionally fine woman, a
woman with no other fault than a slight incautiousness
of character.

8

Far deeper crimes than this we can forgive to an
artist who knows how to envelop his story in such a
dense and shining atmosphere of poetry. We have
never had a novelist who made so beautiful a use of that
time-vision which is one of the richest resources of the
poet. This is not the faculty of reviving in romantic
tale the glittering figures and events of a time long past.
It is the more elevated and poetic faculty of setting the
plainest figures of today in a perspective of ages, in a
shadowy synthesis that, while it dwarfs the present
scene, yet lends it a grandeur, too, a dignity and a noble
pathos borrowed from those of time itself.

And even deeper magic is sometimes taken on by this
time-vision from the mystery that lies in shadows, the
thick and palpable object being contemplated not in
itself but in the spectral copy of itself drawn by the sun
upon some face of wood or stone. It is adding the
mystery of substance to the mystery of time. It is

thus that Hardy shows us the patient row of milkers in the barton sketched on the wall by the lowering summer sun.

There and thus it threw shadows of these obscure and unstudied figures every evening with as much care over each contour as if it had been the profile of a Court beauty on a palace wall; copied them as diligently as it had copied Olympian shapes on marble façades long ago, or the outlines of Alexander, Caesar, and the Pharaohs.

A special element of wonder is added to the daylight wonder of Stonehenge by the way it is approached by Tess and Angel, in the darkness of their furtive midnight journey, and ignorant of their whereabouts. Unable to make out anything by sight, they are guided only by the booming sound of the wind playing upon the gigantic edifice, as it plays upon the Egyptian stones of Memnon, and by the sense of touch which informs them of the shapes of pillar and altar stone. It is with a great shiver of awe that they and the reader come at last to the conclusion that "this pavilion of the night" is Stonehenge, the ancient temple, "older than the centuries; older than the D'Urbervilles."

If anything was needed to give a sense of greater depths of time lying behind them, it was the realization that this edifice was probably dedicated to the worship of the sun. For in this reference back to primitive ritual and myth, one measures time not by years and centuries but by the vast cycles of man's religious sense. Many times in the story of Tess we have this appeal to our ultra-historic imagination: the "old-time heliolatries" being suggested to the author by a hazy sunrise in August, when "the sun, on account of the mist, had a curious sentient, personal look, demanding the masculine pronoun for its adequate expression"; the May-day dance of the women of Marlott being traced to the ancient rites of the local Ceres.

As usual, Hardy is very precise in his notation of those geological diversities that antedate Stonehenge and Cybele, and yet give their present expression to the landscape. There is even more occasion than usual for such science in this book, since the changing fortunes of Tess take her into such various parts of the country, and her sympathetic creator is anxious to make us feel the difference, for example, between the rich alluvial character of the Valley of the Great Dairies, where she spent the days of her happiness and the flinty rudeness of the upland where her life was bitter. In her slow journeys on foot or by wagon, the earthy substructure of the scene is always present to her sense, "perceptible to the tread and to the smell."

Neither she nor her peers are ever seen as other than a part of the landscape. The milkers at the dairy are not merely shadows on the wall of the barton. The barton itself is lost in the meadow in which the buildings are set. "Thus they all worked on, encompassed by the vast flat mead which extended to either slope of the valley—a level landscape compounded of old landscapes long forgotten."

The sense of encompassment by nature is made even stronger by the author's insistence on the remoteness of his scene from the intrusions of civilization. Especially tender is his treatment of the sleepy Vale of Blackmoor and the limited view of the peasant girl for whom this shut-in nook of country is the world. This was "the vale in which she had been born, and in which her life had unfolded. The Vale of Blackmoor was to her the world, and its inhabitants the races thereof. From the gates and stiles of Marlott she had looked down its length in the wondering days of infancy, and what had been mystery to her then was not less than mystery to her now. . . . ."

It is by such means that the figures of the story are all invested with a tender light as of the end of day, with contours softened and every rudeness refined, as in the paintings of Millet or the sculptures of Meunier. It is thus that they sink into the beauty of their setting, at least for us who behold the picture, and half the soreness of life is taken away by the very pathos of their insignificance.

9

It is in *Tess of the D'Urbervilles* that Hardy's pathos culminates—the general envelopment of human nature with his yearning tenderness. It is not merely Tess and her misfortunes that move him. He takes every opportunity of extending his compassionate regard to any creature within his view. He loves to dwell upon the minor solacements which mortals find for anxiety and pain. He dilates more than once upon the comfort of strong drink, which, while it only serves in the long run to deepen trouble, yet for the moment creates an illusion of well-being. Thus he describes the sensations of Mrs. Durbeyfield when she would go to hunt up her shiftless husband at Rolliver's, and "sit there for an hour or two by his side, and dismiss all thought and care of the children during the interval. . . . . A sort of halo, an Occidental glow, came over life then. Troubles and other realities took on themselves a metaphysical impalpability, sinking to mere cerebral phenomena for quiet contemplation." Still more touching, if possible, with its discreet note of irony, is the account of the sensations of the young men and women of Trantridge coming home by moonlight from their revels in the neighboring town. It is just after he has recounted the vulgar quarrel with Tess that Hardy indulges in this description of the idealizing effects of liquor.

And then these children of the open air, whom even excess of alcohol could scarce injure permanently, betook themselves to the field path; and as they went there moved onward with them, around the shadow of each one's head, a circle of opalized light, formed by the moon's rays upon the glittering sheet of dew. Each pedestrian could see no halo but his or her own, which never deserted the head-shadow, whatever its vulgar unsteadiness might be; but adhered to it, and persistently beautified it; till the erratic motions seemed an inherent part of the irradiation, and the fumes of their breathing a component of the night's mist; and the spirit of the scene, and of the moonlight, and of Nature, seemed harmoniously to mingle with the spirit of wine.

But Hardy loves also to dwell on the more healthy solace of nature to sore spirits. He loves to think of Tess, in the time when she hid her shame, watching from under her few square yards of thatch, "winds, and snows, and rains, and gorgeous sunsets, and successive moons at their full." He loves to think of her as taking her solitary walk at the exact moment of evening "when the light and the darkness are so evenly balanced that the constraint of day and the suspense of night neutralize each other, leaving absolute mental liberty," when "the plight of being alive becomes attenuated to its least possible dimensions." And he must have taken a sad joy in her moment of satisfaction when she lay before daybreak upon the stone altar of Stonehenge. . . . . "I like very much to be here," she murmured. "It is so solemn and lonely—after my great happiness— with nothing but the sky above my face. It seems as if there were no folk in the world but we two. . . . ."

And so it is that the poet throws about his pitiful creatures the purple mantle of his compassion. And we can almost forget the pain of the story in its loveliness. The rage and indignation pass; the tenderness remains. And if we say, how pitiful! it is to say, in the next breath, how beautiful!

IX. TRUTH

In *Tess of the D'Urbervilles* it is the simple pathos of
the story that makes the main appeal, and almost
completely takes the place of complication and surprise
as guiding principle and source of interest. In *Jude
the Obscure* the guiding principle and source of interest
are found in pitiless and searching truth. Not but what
Mr. Hardy had generally been a truth-teller, particularly
in regard to human nature, and not least in *Tess*. And
not but what *Jude* is a sufficiently sad story from
beginning to end. But there is here an intensity and
single-mindedness in following the truth which are
unique in the work of Hardy, and which leave us little
energy for any less scientific emotion. No beauty in
the picture, no heroism in character or action is allowed
for a moment to divert us from the pursuit of this grim
quarry.

I

Jude the Obscure is the history of a young man who
grows up in a little village from which at night he can
see in the distance the lights of Christminster (Oxford).
Under the influence of an admired teacher, he early
conceives the idea of going to the university town and
living the splendid dream-life of a scholar; and he
painfully teaches himself the learned languages while
pursuing the trade of a stone-cutter.

But Jude is weak and without knowledge of life;
and he falls victim to the wiles of a vulgar woman,
whom he marries under the persuasion that he must

save her from disgrace. This is practically the ruin of
his hopes. It is only after they have quarreled and
Arabella has left the country that he manages to make
his way to Christminster, hoping that he may still get
admission to the university and realize his dream. But
the officers of the university give him no encouragement.

At Christminster Jude meets his cousin, Sue Bridehead, as well as his old master Phillotson. These two
he brings together, and Sue becomes an assistant teacher
with Phillotson. Jude, meantime, has fallen in love
with her; but, as a married man, he cannot make
advances, and he grows despondent when he finds that
Phillotson is making love to her. He gets drunk,
disgraces himself in a tavern, and returns to Marygreen,
an acknowledged failure. He gives up his dream of
being a scholar, and determines to be a mere curate,
a humble man of religion.

The first of his aspirations has failed, largely because
of Arabella; the second is destined to failure through
the other woman. Jude now goes to live at Melchester
(Salisbury), where Sue is a pupil at a Teachers' Training
School. He works at his trade, and studies faithfully
his Greek New Testament. Sue is engaged to marry
Phillotson, planning to be his helper in teaching after
she has completed her course. Jude has never had the
courage to tell her of his being married; and the two
cousins see much of one another, and live on terms of
sentimental intimacy, leading eventually, through an
accident, to her being compromised and dismissed from
the Training School. It is only then that Jude tells
Sue of Arabella; and soon after she marries Phillotson.
But their union turns out badly; and the generous

husband releases the wife who cannot endure his embraces, finally setting her free by getting a divorce. Meantime she has gone to live with Jude, and this is the cause of his giving up his dream of being a Christian priest: such a profession is inconsistent with his unholy love.

There are still left for Jude the ordinary joys of life, with the love of Sue. But even these he is destined to miss. And the rest of the story is one of gradual degradation and discouragement, leading to a miserable death.

Sue Bridehead is a strange creature. She is devoted to Jude, happy to live with him; but she will be neither his wife nor his mistress. It is only the return of Arabella from Australia and the fear of losing Jude that makes her yield to his passion, and then (when he has divorced Arabella) make an effort to marry him. I say effort; for, with the best of intentions, these lovers cannot bring themselves to enter what seems to them the sordid estate of legal matrimony. And they have to pay the penalty of social ostracism, which drives them to a miserable itinerant life.

But Jude has never quite given up his dream of the scholarly life; and they drift back at last to Christminster, where is played out the last act of Jude's tragedy. They have now three children, the oldest being the son of Jude and Arabella, born in Australia. He is a precocious child, who looks upon life with all the pessimism of disillusioned maturity. He realizes that he and his brothers are a cause of trouble to their parents; and when he learns from Sue that there is to be another baby, he takes matters into his own hands and puts an end to the lives of himself and brothers.

Sue is thereupon smitten with remorse, and imagines this to be a stroke of heaven upon them for their sins. All the time that Jude has known her she has been a thorough rationalist, an unbeliever, and one who regards marriage as a human, an unnecessary, and degrading arrangement. She has even brought about the conversion of Jude to these advanced views. But now she suffers a complete revulsion to the religious and even High Church sentiment of earlier days. Marriage she comes to regard as a holy and sacramental bond which cannot be dissolved: she is still, in the eyes of God, the wife of Phillotson. And back to him she goes, at first to be his companion only, but at last, with great loathing, to make the supreme sacrifice of wifely duty.

Jude, being sick and in despair, falls once again into the clutches of Arabella. Once again he is tricked into marrying her, this time with the help of strong drink. But his health is gone, and he has not long to live. He dies alone while Arabella is enjoying herself on a university holiday; the sounds of an organ concert at one of the colleges and the cheering from the Remembrance games drifting in at his window as he whispers the terrible words of Scripture, "Let the day perish wherein I was born, and the night in which it was said, 'There is a man child conceived.' . . . . Wherefore is light given to him that is in misery, and life unto the bitter in soul?" And while he lies dead at home, Arabella is being embraced by a quack doctor, a man as vulgar as herself.

That is the end of Jude, who dreamed of being a priest and scholar, one of the company of Paley and Butler, of Keble and Pusey and Newman.

2

The bare recital of the main facts of the story in outline will give the reader some notion of the realism of this work; but only the text itself will make him feel the deliberate and uncompromising spirit in which the author followed out his purpose. Not merely has he declined to avail himself of the poetry of the Wessex background which goes so far to mitigate the sadness of earlier stories; he insists on forcing upon us the dreary prose of town and country seen in their least prepossessing light. He wanted to present in vivid contrast the beauty of Jude's aspirations and the ugliness of the actual circumstances of his life. And this ugliness he felt bound to present not merely on its moral side but in the physical detail which makes a kind of symbolic counterpart.

The woman who first ensnares the would-be sage is a coarse and undistinguished daughter of a pig breeder; and she first attracts his attention, while engaged with other girls in washing chitterlings in a brook, by throwing at him for obscene token a "lump of offal" from her butcher's meat. The whole setting of her home, the scene of her wooing, is sordid in the extreme, type of the purely animal love which is destined so ironically to shackle Jude in the pursuits of the mind. And when Jude comes to tell the story later to the woman he loves, the companion of his spirit, the author has chosen for setting a filthy market-place, where "they walked up and down over a floor littered with rotten cabbage leaves, and amid all the usual squalors of decayed vegetable matter and unsalable refuse."

Nowhere in the work of Mr. Hardy—nowhere before perhaps in English fiction—had the subject of sex been

treated in a manner so little colored by romantic convention. It was essential to his theme to set forth the
affair of Arabella altogether free from the glamor of
sentiment. There was here to be none of the deference
to the reader's sensibilities shown in *Tess*. The woman
in the case was "a complete and substantial female
human—no more, no less." She set out deliberately to
catch a man by sexual incitements, and to cheat him
into marrying her by false representations. Nor was
it on his side what we call "love" that thus caught
and lamed him. It was something that

seemed to care little for his reason and his will, nothing for his
so-called elevated intentions, and moved him along, as a violent
school-master a school-boy he has seized by the collar, in a direction which tended towards the embrace of a woman for whom he
had no respect, and whose life had nothing in common with his
own except locality.

What many readers will find most offensive of all is
the absence of even that Puritan moral sentiment which
may indeed consent to record such facts, but solely for
the purpose of condemnation. The author does not
even allow himself the shudder of disgust. The affair
is not indeed related in a tone of comedy, like certain
of the adventures of Tom Jones. But the manner is
equally remote from that of Richardson. Jude is no
different from other men, except as his aspirations are
higher and his sensibilities more fine than the ordinary,
so that the results of his weakness are to injure him more
in his feelings and his career. He is not treated as a
vicious person, but as the subject of a material force
which, working physiologically, is a drag upon his spirit.
If any wrong is imputed, it is to the social requirement of

marriage in a case having so little to do with permanent moral relations.

There seemed to him, vaguely and dimly, something wrong in a social ritual which made necessary a cancelling of well-formed schemes involving years of thought and labor, of foregoing a man's one opportunity of showing himself superior to the lower animals, and of contributing his units to the general progress of his generation, because of a momentary surprise by a new and transitory instinct which had nothing in it of the nature of vice, and could be only at the most called weakness.

And this might be pardoned or even approved by certain earnest readers who cannot pardon the later relapses of Jude. Those who are willing to acknowledge that the instinct in question may be transitory, and even have nothing in it of the nature of vice, may yet be most strenuous in the denial of any possibility that such a man as Jude—so fine, so high-minded—could be caught again, as he was by Arabella, and at times when his sentiment was all, however hopelessly, engaged by Sue.

And then—for there are as many ways of offending in the treatment of sex as there are varieties of temperament—another class of readers may be willing to accept the whole story of Arabella, as at least *natural*, who will repudiate all that relates to Sue as tainted with morbidity and going beyond all decent bounds of frankness. Morbid and unnatural they will find the epicene nature of this woman, whom Jude calls "a distinct type," a creature "intended by Nature to be left intact." Indecently frank and revolting they will find the author's mention (however delicately phrased) of her relation to her husband, her loathing of his contact, and her final sacrifice to what she conceives her religious duty.

Nor is the "disagreeable" character of the book confined to the physical realism and the moral realism in the treatment of sex. If that is of a nature to arouse disgust in many readers, the general outlook on human destiny is of a character more discouraging, more withering to faith and hope. The death of little Father Time and his brothers is in a grimmer vein, grim and austere to the point of tragedy. And the more so as it is deliberately made to typify the spirit of the time, the rooted *maladie du siècle*. "The doctor says there are such boys springing up amongst us," says Jude— "boys of a sort unknown in the last generation—the outcome of new views of life. They seem to see all its terrors before they have staying power to resist them. He says it is the beginning of the coming universal wish not to live."

This is not a new note in Hardy. He has long been occupied with what he takes to be the special cast of modern thought. And years before, in *The Native*, in his account both of Egdon Heath and of Clym Yeobright, he referred to the more sober taste in art which is coming in with the gloomier outlook upon life.

In Clym Yeobright's face could be seen the typical countenance of the future. Should there be a classic period to art hereafter, its Pheidias may produce such faces. The view of life as a thing to be put up with, replacing that zest for existence which was so intense in early civilizations, must ultimately enter so thoroughly into the constitution of the advanced races that its facial expression will be accepted as a new artistic departure.

But it remained for his last novel to give such fearful embodiment to this idea as to make the naturalism of the earlier books appear as white compared with black.

3

This militant naturalism is one symptom of the preoccupation with a philosophy of life which has already become absorbing in *Tess*, but which does not take full possession until the time of *Jude*. In the earlier books Mr. Hardy has been accustomed to make frequent comment upon the general conditions of life and the ways of destiny. But his first consideration has always been for the story itself, the interesting happenings, the dramatic conflicts, the moving fortunes of his characters. Even in *Tess* the author's reflections rather serve to heighten the pathos than to enlighten us on the general problem involved. It is first in *Jude* that the problem takes rank with the story itself as a subject of interest and excitement, so that at every step we are first and most intensely concerned with the *truth*. It is here for the first time that Mr. Hardy's philosophy becomes a prime consideration in the study of his technique.

The story of Jude is that of a man struggling to realize fine ideals, but struggling vainly against a current too strong for him. In the special fineness of his ideals he is no doubt exceptional; in his weakness, in the oversensitive nature that makes him an easy victim of circumstances, he is not perhaps the average, but he is a type of the modern mind as elsewhere pictured by Mr. Hardy in Clym Yeobright and Angel Clare, and which, in little Father Time, produced the grim catastrophe. And his whole career is but the last and most depressing instance of the lifelong persuasion of Mr. Hardy that the dice of the gods are loaded and man is bound to lose.

Many and various are the terms in which this idea has been expressed. In *A Pair of Blue Eyes*, it appears as "a fancy some people hold, when in a bitter mood, ... that inexorable circumstance only tries to prevent what intelligence attempts." In *The Mayor of Casterbridge*, the author speaks in his own character of "the ingenious machinery contrived by the Gods for reducing human possibilities of amelioration to a minimum." In *Tess*, again in his own words, he speaks of the two opposing forces, "the inherent will to enjoy, and the circumstantial will against enjoyment." And finally in *Jude*, he puts into the mouth of Sue a sweeping statement as to the activity of a hostile power in the lives of her and Jude. "There is something external to us which says, 'You shan't!' First it said, 'You shan't learn!' Then it said, 'You shan't labor!' Now it says, 'You shan't love!'"

It seems clear that Mr. Hardy feels more strongly than most English novelists the strength of the forces against which men have to make their way, and the many chances of failure. The world is for him no "Woods of Westermain," in which it takes but courage and love and intelligence to secure the backing of all the forces of nature. The world is a battleground of forces indifferent or even hostile to men, hard at any rate to understand and to get upon one's side. And life is indeed a struggle for existence.

4

There has been much talk about the fatalism of Hardy, but not so much definition of terms. Fatalism is the mental attitude of one who feels that what happens to us, or what we do, is necessitated by the nature of things or by the decree of some mysterious power over which we have no control. It is an attitude of mind natural to men who have been defeated in their struggle with the world in spite of the best they can do, and who, in their despair of being able to affect the course of things, exclaim with Clym Yeobright, "Well, what must be will be," or with Jude, "Nothing can be done. Things are as they are, and will be brought to their destined issue." Jude was quoting from a chorus of the *Agamemnon.* He was tired of the conflict and ready to give in, not with the religious exaltation of the true fatalist, but with the same surrender to necessity. The peculiar note of fatalism is that it takes no account of the causes which produce a given result. Jude was not by nature a fatalist, though he may have been a determinist.

The determinist may be equally impressed with the helplessness of man in the grip of strange forces, physical and psychical. But he is distinguished from the fatalist by his concern with the causes that are the links in the chain of necessity. Determinism is the scientific counterpart of fatalism, and throws more light on destiny by virtue of its diligence in the searching out of natural law. Mr. Hardy is rather a determinist than a fatalist. When he speaks most directly and unmistakably for himself, it is to insist on the universal working of the laws of cause and effect. "That she had chosen for her afternoon walk the road along which she had returned to Casterbridge three hours earlier in a carriage was curious—if anything should be called curious in *a concatenation of phenomena wherein each is known to have its accounting cause.*"

The point in which determinism and fatalism agree is the helplessness of the individual will against the will in things. Only the determinist conceives the will in things as the sum of the natural forces with which we have to cope, whereas the fatalist tends to a more religious interpretation of that will as truly and literally a *will*, an arbitrary power, a personal force like our own. Sometimes Mr. Hardy allows his characters the bitter comfort of that personal interpretation. "Henchard, like all his kind, was superstitious, and he could not help thinking that the concatenation of events this evening had produced was *the scheme of some sinister intelligence bent on punishing him. Yet they had developed naturally.*" It was so that Eustacia Vye, wishing to escape the responsibility for the shutting out of Mrs. Yeobright, imagines a spiritual power upon whom to put it. "Instead of blaming herself for the issue she laid the fault upon the shoulders of some indistinct, colossal Prince of the World, who had framed her situation and ruled her lot."

What gives rise to such notions is the ironic discrepancy between what we seek and what we secure, between what we do and what follows from it. We have control of so very few of the factors that go to determine our fortunes that we can hardly help imagining behind the scene a capricious and malignant contriver of contretemps. It is generally to his characters that Mr. Hardy ascribes such interpretations. Thus in *A Pair of Blue Eyes*, he tells us that, to the West Country folk,

Nature seems to have moods in other than a poetical sense; predilections for certain deeds at certain times, without any apparent law to govern or season to account for them. She is read as a person with a curious temper; as one who does not scatter kindnesses and cruelties alternately, but heartless severities and overwhelming generosities in lawless caprice.

And sometimes the author lets *himself* fall into a manner of speaking not strictly scientific. It is true that the order of nature is one that does not regard the wishes of men; that what we are after and what nature is after make two distinct systems, which often enough interfere and collide to our distress and bewilderment. And it is hard for the most sober of writers to find terms of prose for expressing what is a general and legitimate philosophical notion—that of the sum of forces with which we have to reckon. Mr. Hardy is not the most sober of writers, but a poet of ·ivid imagination, a satirist intensely conscious of the incongruities in the nature of things. Is it not natural that he should speak, in reflective mood, of "Nature's tr acherous attempt to put an end to" Knight upon the c iff? of "the waggery of fate which started Clive as a writing clerk" and "banished the wild and ascetic h :ath lad [Clym] to a trade whose sole concern was with the especial symbols of self-indulgence and vainglory"? of "an unsympathetic First Cause" which allowed Tess but one chance in life?—and that he should speak with tears of indignation in his voice of "the President of the Immortals" and "his sport with Tess"? He is but using the handy personifications by which we all attempt to characterize as a whole the principle lying behind the action of natural law. He does not mean to say that Nature is a lady with evil designs upon Mr. Knight, or to predicate the existence of a deity bent on torturing Tess. He is neither a fatalist nor one urging belief in the governance of God.

It is true that Mr. Hardy does give us a more than usual sense of the mysterious and inscrutable character of destiny. And this is partly from his use of poetic imagery drawn from religion. "The ways of the maker are dark." According to one of the most penetrating of his critics, "C'est ce pouvoir de suggérer le mystère métaphysique, si nous pouvons parler ainsi, derrière les actes les plus ordinaires, qui donne aux œuvres de M. Hardy leur cachet particulier et distingue leur auteur des autres romanciers de son époque."[1] But, more and more as he goes on, Mr. Hardy makes it clear that it is not really a metaphysical mystery that lies behind his tragic stories, but the wholly natural mystery of maladjustments in the very nature of things. It might all be summed up in that highly imaginative— but in no way "metaphysical"—account in *Tess* of "the universal harshness" out of which grow the particular harshnesses of men with women and women with men. These harshnesses, he says, "are tenderness itself when compared with the universal harshness out of which they grow; the harshness of the position towards the temperament, of the means towards the aims, of to-day towards yesterday, of hereafter towards to-day."

One must not overlook the accent of irony in his use of terms for the divinity. He takes frequent occasion to insinuate his scorn of the unthinking optimism of an easy faith. It is this perhaps which leads to his championing of Eustacia against the Supreme Power which had placed "a being of such exquisite finish . . . . in circumstances calculated to make of her charms a curse

---

[1] F. A. Hedgcock, *Thomas Hardy, Penseur et Artiste* (Paris), p. 172.

rather than a blessing." And this ironic reaction to the prevailing religious optimism is perhaps responsible for his one covert suggestion of a First Cause "of lower moral quality than [our] own." He may have been reading the posthumous essay of J. S. Mill in which are presented the possible alternatives (granting the existence of God) of a deity benevolent but not all-powerful and a deity all-powerful but not benevolent. But this must not be taken as more than the momentary fling of a spirit made somewhat sour by the sweetness of Victorian sentiment.

5

But there does remain one practice of Mr. Hardy which is liable to give rise to the impression of his being a fatalist. Mr. Hedgcock in particular is impressed with the fatalistic cast given to so many of his novels by the large use in them of accident and coincidence, forcing the hands of the characters, taken together with the use of personifications like those mentioned above. But the two things are not necessarily connected. It is not in the novels in which he has contrived most ingeniously a fatal chain of causes that he has the most to say of the First Cause or the Supreme Power. The forced sequences of surprising event in *Two on a Tower*, the bizarre recurrences of identical situations in *The Well-Beloved*, are almost wholly unaccompanied by any reflection upon the guiding principle of the universe; while it is in *Tess*, almost entirely free from the intrusion of accident, that the author dilates upon the activity of "an unsympathetic First Cause," upon "cruel Nature's law" and "the circumstantial will against enjoyment," and takes his final fling at the sport of "the President of the Immortals."

Again, it is in some of the stories in which the largest part is played by accident and coincidence that Mr. Hardy makes the most unqualified assertions of the reign of natural law. It is in *Casterbridge*, with its apparently fatal chain of occurrences, that he insists most on the law of cause and effect in the concatenation of events. In *Two on a Tower* and *The Well-Beloved* the few philosophical references to be found are to the processes of nature.

The excessive use of accident and coincidence by Mr. Hardy seems to have been from motives of art rather than philosophy. It is not so much to illustrate a theory of life as for the sake of an interesting plot that he tangles up his characters in such a web of circumstance. This is obvious enough in a book like *A Laodicean*, where the outcome is happy, and where the complications and difficulties serve, as in any romance, as hurdles for the hero and heroine to clear in their race for happiness.

And as the aim is artistic rather than philosophical, so does the objection lie rather on grounds of art than on grounds of truth.

Everyone knows, as a matter of daily experience, that we have not complete control of our fortunes, that the general order of events is constantly interfering with our particular set of aims. An accident is simply a happening in the general order which comes to favor us or to upset our calculations. It intrudes upon our order with the shock and disaster of the housewife's broom sweeping away a spider's web. It is, as Hardy

expresses it, in reference to a misfortune of the Durbeyfields, a thing which comes upon us "irrespective of
will, or law, or desert, or folly; a *chance external impinge-
ment* to be borne with; not a lesson." There can be no
objection on grounds of truth to the recording of such
accidents.

But on the other hand, they can have little value
for literary art. For they have no moral significance;
they throw no light upon human nature or the social
order. And they are accordingly just so much waste
material, just so much of a weight for the author to
carry. If such an accident is a major event, it has to
be set forth at some length; it has to be accounted for.
And that takes a portion of the author's precious time,
of the reader's precious store of energy. If there are
many such events, and much complication of the action,
the story becomes unwieldy; the author has not space
to turn round in, as Henry James would express it.
The true subjects of his study must be neglected for
tiresome and unilluminating explanations. The miracle
of *The Mayor of Casterbridge* is that, with such a stagger-
ing burden of overhead expenses in the way of mere
plot, the author can still pay dividends on the income
from character.

6

There is a great difference between positive interfer-
ence from the external order in the shape of unfortunate
accident, and a mere failure to favor the hopes of men.
It is chiefly in the latter form that the hostility or
indifference of nature shows itself in the later novels.
Thus in *Jude*, when the boy was so painfully devoting
himself to the learning of Latin and Greek, the author

remarks that somebody might have come along to help
him in his difficulties. "But nobody did come, because
nobody does." This is, of course, the very opposite of
coincidence; it is a denial of all the marvels of romance,
always on the lookout for angel or knight-errant to
save one from the dungeon of ennui and incompetence.

Of the same character is that want of design in the
adjustment of the man to the hour, etc., of which Mr.
Hardy expatiates so at length apropos of the affair of
Tess and Alec.

> In the ill-judged execution of the well-judged plan of things
> the call seldom produces the comer, the man to love rarely coin-
> cides with the hour for loving. Nature does not often say "See!"
> to a poor creature at a time when seeing can lead to happy doing;
> or reply "Here!" to a body's cry of "Where?" till the hide-and-
> seek has become an irksome, outworn game. . . . . In the present
> case, as in millions, the two halves of an approximately perfect
> whole did not confront each other at the perfect moment; part
> and counterpart wandered independently about the earth in the
> stupidest manner for a while, till the late time came. . . . .

Here is no accident, no coincidence, no fatal chain of
events, no case of skilful and ingenious contrivance on
the part of destiny. Here is simply a total want of any
contrivance for the benefit of the human beings concerned. It is but a *negative* hostility, or indifference, of
the external order, which is here displayed; and there
is no objection to be entered in the interest either of
truth or of art.

7

But when it comes to *positive motivation*, it is generally better art to ignore altogether the operations and
dispositions of an extra-human order, which are so hard

to trace and chart, and confine one's self to familiar human nature. Only so can one avoid the arbitrary and freakish, and leave one's self free to study the significant and humanly interesting. If we must have a villain, or antagonist, outside the rôle of the characters, let it be that odious abstraction, Society, or Convention. It is largely so in both *Tess* and *Jude;* and that is why these novels have so very modern a tone among the works of a somewhat old-fashioned writer. If Nature is sometimes referred to in these books as a cruel step-mother, she more often appears as an enlightened champion against the obscurantism of Social Convention. In *Tess* it is to the convention of the "fallen woman" that Mr. Hardy opposes the now familiar figure of the really "pure" woman become the victim of a natural instinct, and then the more pitiful victim of the "fallen woman" superstition.

In *Jude* the great antagonist is the institution of marriage, especially in its sacramental High Church aspect. Marriage appears as a mischief-maker in the cases of both Jude and Sue; and in Jude's case it was both in relation to Arabella and to Sue. It was a disastrous mistake for him to marry Arabella in deference to the social convention of legalizing their union, of making her "an honest woman." His life was ruined by the fundamental error of basing "a permanent contract on a temporary feeling which had no necessary connection with affinities that alone render a life-long comradeship tolerable." He was permanently crippled in his career as a scholar. And what was left of hope and idealism was nullified by the illegality and impiety of his later passion for Sue.

Strange that his first aspiration—towards academical proficiency—had been checked by a woman, and that his second aspiration—towards apostleship—had also been checked by a woman. "Is it," he said, "that the women are to blame; or is it *the artificial system of things*, under which the normal sex-impulses are turned into devilish domestic gins and springes to noose and hold back those who want to progress?"

As for Sue, her misery in the wedded state is equally attributed to a contravention of nature. "It is none of the natural tragedies of love," she says, rather sententiously, "that's love's usual tragedy in civilized life, but a tragedy artificially manufactured for people who in a natural state would find relief in parting." Throughout the book there is much irony in the treatment of the marriage vow, on the part both of the characters and of the author.

And so, standing before the aforesaid officiator, the two swore that at every other time of their lives they would assuredly believe, feel, and desire precisely as they had believed, felt, and desired during the few preceding weeks. What was as remarkable as the undertaking itself was the fact that nobody seemed at all surprised at what they swore.

There is a frequent suggestion in the talk of Jude and Sue of the "advanced" modern views of marriage. But in the end Sue underwent a change of heart; and it was the sacerdotal view of marriage as an indissoluble bond which led her back to Phillotson and brought about the final sordid ending.

8

Whatever is done in deference to convention or upon religious conviction is done in accordance with human nature itself. And such motivation is well within the circle of familiar psychology, completely shut off from the world of accident external to our wills. Much of the action in *Jude* again is to be referred not to conventional or religious motives taken by themselves, but to the interaction between them and instincts simply human and natural.

Quite the most interesting parts of the story, and those which meet best that ideal of scenic representation which reigns in *Tess* and *The Native*, are the long series of scenes between Jude and Sue in the third and fourth books, and again in the last book, in which the ticklish uncertainty of their relation is exhibited in long-drawn-out dialogues of great intensity of feeling. Even before Jude has told Sue of his being married, these scenes have begun. Jude is in love with Sue, but conscious of being fettered by his marriage to Arabella. Sue is half in love with Jude. She loves to be loved, and is unusually sensitive to indifference or disapproval. But she does not want to go too far. She does not want a love affair. And besides, she is engaged to Phillotson, not to speak of the cousinship with Jude, and the long tradition of marital unhappiness in their family. And so their commerce is one continuous succession of advances and retreats on one part or the other, of little quarrels and ardent reconciliations. Sue takes everything in so personal a way! She is so easily hurt, and must be comforted! She so hates to be thought conventional, and so longs for tenderness and intimacy! Jude is hurt on his side by her callous rationalism in the treatment of his religious beliefs; and then she must hasten to make up for her want of considerateness. She is always parting from him in coldness, and then writing him the warmest of notes. They are both so easily made jealous! There is so much excitement in their handclasp; so much emotion in her contralto throat-note under stress of feeling; and then: "She looked up trustfully, and her voice seemed trying to nestle in his breast."

The climax of these scenes of cat-and-mouse playing with love comes in the fourth book, after her marriage to Phillotson, when Jude and Sue meet at Marygreen for the funeral of their Aunt Drusilla. It is impossible, short of quoting the long dialogue, to give a notion of the tense dramatic play of feeling between them, as Sue suggests the hypothetical problem of a woman with a physical aversion to her husband, and then arrives at a confession of her own unhappiness with the schoolmaster—how Jude guesses she is unhappy and she denies it; how Jude's religious doctrines are at variance with his instinct in the matter; how for each concession to the tenderness between them they have to put forward the justification of cousinship, or that of innocent consolation, which provokes a corresponding reaction of jealousy; and so on and on through rising degrees of agony. Even after they have said goodnight, the cry of a wounded animal brings them together again. Jude is wakened by the squeak of a rabbit, and goes out to give it release from its pain. And so he comes to talk with Sue, who is also troubled by the rabbit, and whom he finds looking out of the open casement. There is no reference between them to what must have been for both the symbolic character of the trapped beast. But there is more talk of her unhappiness and his doctrines; there is kissing of hands; and finally, "in a moment of impulse she bent over the sill, and laid her face upon his hair, weeping." It was not, however, until the following day that Jude and Sue yielded at last to the passion they had so long held away from them. Upon her departure from Marygreen an incident occurred.

> They had stood parting in the silent highway, and their tense and passionate moods had led to bewildered inquiries of each other on how far their intimacy ought to go; till they had almost quarrelled, and she had said tearfully that it was hardly proper of him as a parson in embryo to think of such a thing as kissing her even in farewell, as he now wished to do. Then she had conceded that the fact of the kiss would be nothing; all would depend upon the spirit of it. If given in the spirit of a cousin and a friend, she saw no objection; if in the spirit of a lover, she could not permit it. "Will you swear that it will not be in that spirit?" she had said.
>
> No; he would not. And then they had turned from each other in estrangement, and gone their several ways, till at a distance of twenty or thirty yards both had looked round simultaneously. That look behind was fatal to the reserve hitherto more or less maintained. They had quickly run back, and met, and embracing most unpremeditatedly, kissed each other. When they parted for good it was with flushed cheeks on her side, and a beating heart on his.[1]

It is a pity that Mr. Hardy should have seen fit to give thus in *summary*—in the tame pluperfect—what might have been, in full presentation in dialogue form, the most moving scene in all his work. But we ought not to complain, considering that we have, in the scenes that go before, and in those that follow, almost the greatest treasure of dramatic dialogue which he or any other English novelist has bestowed upon us.

[1] Pp. 256-57.

The scenes that follow, on the train and in the hotel at Aldbrickham, bring into prominence an element in the character of Sue which cannot be blamed upon convention, since Nature is made solely responsible for it. She was "intended by Nature to be left intact"; and however much she may crave to be loved, it is only with extreme reluctance that she can give herself even to Jude, whom she loves. It is only remotely that this affects the problem of the book; but it does contribute to the artistic interest by prolonging the scenes of tension between her and Jude.

It is her reluctance to go through the ceremony of marriage, after she has been divorced from Phillotson, that brings upon her and Jude the condemnation of the world; and so we come again to the opinion of the world—to the "conventions" and "moral hobgoblins" —as the provoking cause of the action. It is this which causes the death of the children, and all that follows. The great drama of the final book lies in the renewed strain between Jude and Sue owing to her conversion back to the religious point of view. And now recurs, on the altar steps of St. Silas and at her chamber door, the harrowing alternation of sternness and tenderness in her treatment of Jude that makes the drama of this relentless history.

9

Seldom had Mr. Hardy drawn his effects so straight from human nature. It is true that he is keenly conscious here, as in *Tess* and in *The Native*, of this and that "flaw in the terrestrial scheme." But these flaws, in so far as they affect the action of the story, are found in character itself, or in the social arrangements which are the collective expression of the will of men. Jude and Sue are both frankly represented as humanly weak, as more than ordinarily sensitive to pain, and ill adapted to an order that calls for a certain callousness as a condition of survival. They and the children are living in a world which does not want them. Sue is perhaps to be regarded as a positively morbid type. But such perversity of character is a very different thing from that perversity in things themselves which breeds capricious and unaccountable accident and weaves a web of fatal events "irrespective of will, or law, or desert, or folly." And for the most part, the action is the clear and inevitable outcome of the social order of which the characters are a part, now as rebels and now as more or less loyal subjects. So that everything that happens is characteristic and full of meaning.

It is true that we have a fairly liberal allowance of major happenings to be disposed of: marriage, divorce, remarriage, and death. But there is an almost complete absence of those minor complications so much in evidence in *Two on a Tower* and *The Mayor of Casterbridge*, even in so fine a work as *The Native*. There are no intrusions from without; everything comes about naturally from the stated conditions of the problem. And none of the author's precious time must be wasted upon the setting of traps and the unraveling of mysteries. The pattern is large and bold, but simple and unforced; and each development in the plot is followed through in leisurely fashion and with satisfying amplitude of detail.

Many readers will put *Jude* above *Tess* as a work of art. It is clearly not so beautiful. For one thing, the author has denied himself the glamor and richness of the Wessex background, a want but ill supplied by the insubstantial rainbow vision of Christminster. And then the characters themselves are not of the same radiant and heroic mold as Tess and Angel Clare. They are the stunted growth of modern life, with all its maladjustment, discontent, and restless, craving intellectuality. They are poor creatures of an urban industrial order. Beside the ordinary characters of English fiction, and in the light of Victorian poetry, they carry a strong suggestion of the pathological. The first instinct of a reader coming to these two novels from his Tennyson and Browning, his Thackeray and Meredith, is greatly to prefer the melodious pathos and undimmed idealism of *Tess*.

But later impressions do better justice to *Jude*. We find ourselves more and more gripped by the plain truthfulness of the record. Upon reflection, we like the complete freedom from melodramatic features like the seduction of Tess and the murder of Alec. In the persons of Jude and Sue we recognize the human nature of our unheroic experience. We follow the course of their lives with a breathless suspense not so much over what shall happen to them as what the truth shall prove to be. This is the note of the time that was coming in. The reader fresh from Ibsen and Flaubert and Tolstoi may even prefer the drab and biting realism of *Jude* to the shimmering poetry of *Tess*. He will probably find it to be a more characteristic expression of the time.

10

It stands in any case as one of the three great achievements of the art of Thomas Hardy. Mr. Hardy as a novelist was liable to a kind of diabolic possession by the demon of plot.[1]   He was forever being ridden and led astray by the very British notion that a story, to be interesting, must be complicated and full of exciting events.   In several cases he found release from this obsession by yielding himself to the control of some brighter spirit, some power that made for simplicity and naturalness as well as for a more profoundly human appeal.   In each case the result more than justified his tardy boldness in abandoning the antiquated machinery of his trade.   *The Return of the Native, Tess of the D'Urbervilles*, and *Jude the Obscure* prove to be the most interesting as well as the best made of his novels.   Art and craft were in their fashioning identical.   It is not always perhaps that the relative appeal of a novelist's works is so directly in proportion to their relative excellence in technique.

[1] I have recently received comfort and support in this view of the matter by an opinion expressed by Mr. Edward Garnett in his *Friday Nights*.   Mr. Garnett is particularly impressed in the case of *The Mayor of Casterbridge* with the damage done to Hardy's art by overcomplication of plot.

BIBLIOGRAPHICAL NOTE

BIBLIOGRAPHICAL NOTE

The fullest and most satisfactory bibliography of Thomas Hardy is that by A. P. Webb, published by Frank Hollings, London, 1916, and in the same year by the Torch Press, Cedar Rapids, Iowa. This book contains a full description, up to the year of publication, of "First Editions," of "Nugae and Privately Printed Books," and of "The Wessex Novels"; together with lists of Mr. Hardy's "Contributions to Books," his "Contributions to Periodicals and Newspapers," lists of "Critical Notices, Essays, and Appreciations [of Hardy's work] in Books, and in Periodicals," a list of plays based on his books, and an appendix describing certain autographed poems of Hardy. In the same year appeared Henry Danielson's *The First Editions of the Writings of Thomas Hardy and Their Values: a Bibliographical Handbook for Collectors, Booksellers, Librarians and Others*, published by Allen and Unwin. And still in this same year of 1916 there appeared, as appendix to Harold Child's *Thomas Hardy* ("Writers of the Day Series," London: Nisbet; Boston: Holt), "A Short Bibliography of Thomas Hardy's Principal Works," by Arundell Esdaile, together with a brief American bibliography.

Mr. Esdaile briefly describes the collected editions. These include: (1) The Wessex Novels, a series begun by Osgood, McIlvaine and Co. in 1895, and continued successively by Harpers and Macmillan, with the volumes of poems uniform, a series which "may be considered as still in progress"; (2) new and cheaper Uniform Edition,

1902, etc., "the familiar 3s. 6d. edition in blue-grey covers, with the map of Wessex," Macmillan (in America, Harpers); (3) Pocket Edition, 1906, etc., "a re-issue on small India paper, of the Uniform Edition" (Macmillan, Harpers); (4) Wessex Edition, *The Works of Thomas Hardy*, 1912, etc., with a general Preface, "containing the author's revisions," including several volumes of verse, and the Wessex Novels rearranged as: "I. Novels of Character and Environment," "II. Romances and Fantasies," "III. Novels of Ingenuity," "IV. Mixed Novels." As for the "author's revisions," by the way, the reader should be warned that many such were introduced in several of the earlier editions. References in my text are to number (2) above, with which, I believe, the paging of (3) is identical.

The only important volumes by Thomas Hardy, not reprints of earlier work, published since 1916 are *Moments of Vision and Miscellaneous Verses*, Macmillan, 1917, and *Late Lyrics and Earlier, with Many Other Verses*, Macmillan, 1922. His *Collected Poems* were published in one volume by Macmillan in 1919, *Selected Poems* ("Golden Treasury Series," Macmillan) appeared in 1916. The epic-drama of *The Dynasts* (originally 1903, 1906, 1908) was published in a single volume by Macmillan in 1920. Certain special American editions of novels may be mentioned as follows: *The Return of the Native*, edited with introduction by Professor J. W. Cunliffe, Scribner, 1917; *The Mayor of Casterbridge*, with introduction by Joyce Kilmer, Modern Library of the World's Best Books, Boni and Liveright, 1917; *Far from the Madding Crowd*, with introduction by Professor William T. Brewster, Harpers, 1918.

The most important studies of Hardy are the following: *The Art of Thomas Hardy*, by Lionel Johnson, Lane, 1894; *Essai de Critique: Thomas Hardy, Penseur et Artiste*, by F. C. Hedgcock, Paris, 1911; and *Thomas Hardy, a Critical Study*, by Lascelles Abercrombie, Martin Secker, 1912. Since 1916, the following volumes have appeared: *Thomas Hardy: a Study of the Wessex Novels*, by H. C. Duffin, Longmans, first edition, 1916, second edition, with an appendix on the poems and *The Dynasts*, 1921; *Thomas Hardy: Poet and Novelist*, by Samuel C. Chew, "Bryn Mawr Notes and Monographs," Longmans, 1921; *Thomas Hardy: the Artist, the Man and the Disciple of Destiny*, by A. Stanton Whitfield, Grant Richards, 1921. Other volumes since 1916 devoted in part to Hardy are: *George Eliot and Thomas Hardy*, by L. W. Berle, Kennerley, 1917; *Moderns*, (pp. 103–59), by John Freeman, Crowell, 1917; *English Literature during the Last Half Century*, by J. W. Cunliffe, Macmillan, 1919.

I will add for the convenience of students a list of the novels with dates of first publication both in book and in periodical form.

CHRONOLOGICAL LIST OF THE NOVELS

1871. *Desperate Remedies*. Tinsley 3 vols.

1872. *Under the Greenwood Tree*. Tinsley 3 vols.

1872–73. *A Pair of Blue Eyes*. *Tinsley's Magazine*, September, 1872, to July, 1873.
—1873. Tinsley 3 vols.

1874. *Far from the Madding Crowd*. *Cornhill Magazine*, January to December.
—1874. Smith, Elder 2 vols.

1875–76. *The Hand of Ethelberta*. *Cornhill Magazine*, July, 1875, to May, 1876.
—1876. Smith, Elder 2 vols.

1878.   *The Return of the Native.* *Belgravia*, January to December.
          —1878. Smith, Elder 3 vols.
1880.   *The Trumpet-Major.* *Good Words*, January to December.
          —1880. Smith, Elder 3 vols.
1880–81. *A Laodicean.* *Harper's Magazine*, European Edition, December, 1880, to December, 1881.
          —1881. Sampson, Low, Marston and Co. 3 vols.
1882.   *Two on a Tower.* *Atlantic Monthly*, January to December.
          —1882. Sampson, Low, Marston and Co. 3 vols.
1883.   *The Romantic Adventures of a Milkmaid.* *Graphic*, Summer Number; *Harper's Weekly*, June 23 to August 4.
          —1884. George Munro, 1 vol., paper wrapper. The curious bibliographical history of this little novel is set forth in my note in the *Nation* (New York) XCIV, (1912), 82–83.
1886.   *The Mayor of Casterbridge.* *Graphic*, January 2 to May 15.
          —1886. Smith, Elder 2 vols.
1886–87. *The Woodlanders.* *Macmillan's Magazine*, May, 1886, to April, 1887.
          —1887. Macmillan 3 vols.
1891.   *Tess of the D'Urbervilles.* *Graphic*, July 4 to December 26.
          —1891. Osgood, McIlvaine 3 vols.
1892.   *The Well-Beloved.* Under the title of "The Pursuit of the Well-Beloved," in *Illustrated London News*, October 1 to December 17.
          —1897. Macmillan.
1894–95. *Jude the Obscure.* Under the title of "The Simpletons," in *Harper's New Monthly Magazine*, European Edition, December, 1894. Continued under the title of "Hearts Insurgent" in the same magazine January to November, 1895.
          —1896. Osgood, McIlvaine.

INDEX

INDEX

PRINTED IN THE U.S.A.